TURNING POINTS

15 Pivotal Moments in Nova Scotia's History

Paul W. Bennett

MacIntyre Purcell Publishing Inc.

MacIntyre Purcell Publishing Inc.
194 Hospital Rd.
Lunenburg, Nova Scotia
B0J 2C0
(902) 640-3350

www.macintyrepurcell.com
info@macintyrepurcell.com

Printed and bound in Canada Friesens

Design and layout: Denis Cunningham
Cover design: Denis Cunningham

ISBN: 978-1-77276-118-4

Library and Archives Canada Cataloguing in Publication

Title: Turning points : 15 pivotal moments in Nova Scotia's history / Paul W. Bennett.
Other titles: 15 pivotal moments in Nova Scotia's history | Fifteen pivotal moments in Nova Scotia's history | Chronicle-herald (Halifax, N.S.)
Names: Bennett, Paul W., 1949- author.
Description: A brief survey history identifying pivotal episodes in Nova Scotia's past, based upon a series of special features that originally appeared in The NovaScotian, a supplement to The Chronicle Herald.
Identifiers: Canadiana 2019005350X | ISBN 9781772761184 (softcover)
Subjects: LCSH: Nova Scotia—History.
Classification: LCC FC2311 .B46 2019 | DDC 971.6—dc23

MacIntyre Purcell Publishing Inc. would like to acknowledge the financial support of the Government of Canada and the Nova Scotia Department of Tourism, Culture and Heritage.

"While it is all very well to talk of 'turning points', one can surely only recognize such moments in retrospect."

Kazuo Ishiguro, *The Remains of the Day (1989)*

To Dianne – for making all that I do possible and for allowing me the freedom to roam at-large in the world of ideas.

TABLE OF CONTENTS

Introduction/ Turning Points in History
The Shifting Axis and Nova Scotia's Place in Canada

Nova Scotia has never been a straightforward kind of place. That's how Halifax author John DeMont described the province in his enchanting 2017 book *The Long Way Home*. In that personal memoir, he comes closer than anyone else to explaining the Atlantic province's uniqueness and fathoming its emotional pull for those who call it home. The province's motto, *Munit haec et altera vincit* (One defends and the other conquers), captures well that ethos.

Without an inspiring, onward and upward trajectory, the province and its people have found a way to navigate the ups and downs, twists and turns that come with being, for most of its history, the easternmost appendage of British North America and the Dominion of Canada. Over much of that time, the British colony and later province of Nova Scotia was viewed, by the rest of the world, as a place of new starts, shaped by the sea, full of shimmering landscapes, slightly out-of-step with central Canada and its gospel of material progress.

Looking through a Nova Scotian lens, there's another lesson. We follow a different path and always seem to be, in DeMont's words, "on the cusp of something big." In that sense, we have much to teach the world about how to persevere through periodic struggles and somehow find a way forward.

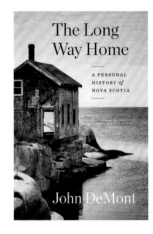

(Above) Cover of John DeMont's memoir, The Long Way Home.

(Below) A monument to Joseph Howe's legacy on the grounds of the Nova Scotia House of Assembly.

AN EASTERN GATEWAY

Nova Scotia was destined, largely by its geography, to be an eastern gateway to the continent en route to somewhere else. For much of its existence, Nova Scotia has bobbed around as a colonial possession at the mercy of European empires and then as a relatively small province in a Dominion bent upon pursuing a westward destiny on this continent.

One of Canada's greatest historians, J.M.S. Careless, aptly described the process as "metropolitanism" advancing from east to west, starting with the dominant commercial centres of Halifax, Quebec and Montreal, but then moving on to Toronto, the metropolis of "Empire Ontario," and points west. Since the Canadian Confederation of 1867, the province has found itself gradually bypassed as the axis of national development shifted from Ontario and Quebec to the West and the Pacific Coast.

If Nova Scotia has a patron saint, it would have to be Joseph Howe, the renowned Halifax journalist, newspaper editor, and politician. While Howe was instrumental in Nova Scotia's movement for Responsible Government and respected for his defense of freedom of the press, he is perhaps best known outside the Maritimes as a fierce Anti- Confederate who opposed the colony's 1867 entry into the Canadian federal union. From his perch at the *Morning Herald*, he blasted away at Confederation as a "Botheration Scheme" and took his case all the way to London in 1866. Leading supporters of Confederation such as Sir Charles Tupper remain largely forgotten, but Howe, the contrarian, lives on in the hearts and minds of Nova Scotians.

(Above) Thomas Chandler Haliburton, author of two-volume 1829 history of Nova Scotia.

"A SMALL PLACE" IN THE EMPIRE

Perceptions and interpretations of Nova Scotia's history have not only changed over time, but reflected a diverse range of historical viewpoints. One of the province's earliest historians, Thomas C. Haliburton, writing in his two-volume 1829 account, cast Nova Scotia within the distinctly Euro centric framework of British imperial expansion into unclaimed lands. Penned almost forty years before Confederation, Haliburton saw Nova Scotia occupying "a small place" in "the great chain of events" associated with the British "discovery" and occupation of the continent.

Steeped in the narrowly white European views of his time, Haliburton saw the story as a small chapter in the slow moving, conquest-by-conquest "progress of man from a state of nature towards civilization." His relative blindness to the existence and cultural sophistication of the Mi'kmaq, Nova Scotia's first inhabitants, is shocking by today's standards.

THE REGIONAL PROTEST TRADITION

Later Maritime regional historians tended to situate Nova Scotia within a regional protest and resistance tradition. Regional disparities loomed large in the analysis of these popular and scholarly historians who sought to explain the sources of the whole region's economic difficulties following Confederation and extending into the post-World War II years. Heavily influenced by the dominance of central Canadian modernizers like Prime Minister Louis St. Laurent's 'Minister of Everything,' C.D. Howe, they focused unduly on the "backwardness" of local people and their institutions. The Atlantic Canadian historian David Frank aptly described that perspective as the "blame the victim syndrome." Nova Scotia, in particular, was painted with the brush of "Maritime conservatism" which dampened entrepreneurial spirit and gave comfort to timidity and dependence among the region's business community.

University of New Brunswick historian Ernie Forbes effectively challenged those long-standing myths in a series of influential books and articles shedding new light on the legitimate grievances of Maritimers and the sources of robust regional identities in Nova Scotia and neighbouring Maritime provinces. A more recent short history of Nova Scotia, John Reid's 2009 *Nova Scotia: A Pocket History*, builds upon Forbes' regional studies, dispels persistent myths of backwardness, and provides a welcome antidote for the kind of historical amnesia that leaves us "stumbling around in the dark."

(Above) An idyllic Nova Scotia sea landscape with that iconic lighthouse.

CANADA'S OCEAN PLAYGROUND ETHOS

Nova Scotia's brand identity is neatly captured on its license plates saluting "Canada's Ocean Playground." Its stunning ocean coastline and crossroads location in the Atlantic world have made it a premier tourist destination for visitors from around the world. From re-enactments at the Halifax Citadel and monuments to the 1917 Explosion and Pier 21 to postcards of Peggy's Cove lighthouse and the Bluenose, the province has cultivated a thriving tourism industry that relies heavily on constructing and marketing the province's history.

In their 2010 book, *In the Province of History*, Ian McKay and Robin Bates probe deeply into provincial promotional ventures from the time of Henry Wadsworth Longfellow's 1847 epic poem *Evangeline* until well into the 20th century. Nova Scotia's Scottish tradition, touted by Premier Angus L. Macdonald and dubbed "tartanism" is depicted as a fabrication rooted in "folklore" and "commodified" for tourism purposes. Even Halifax's venerated popular historian Thomas Head Raddall is presented as an emissary of a tourist-driven history which celebrates Scottish folk tales and exalts whiteness, while virtually ignoring ethnic minorities, women, and working-class people.

ROMANTIC VISIONS OF NOVA SCOTIANISM

Telling the story of Nova Scotia has also attracted its share of romantics. One of the best of this genre is Lesley Choyce's most entertaining 1996 book, *Nova Scotia: Shaped by the Sea*. Writing with literary flair, he provides a compelling and alluring personal interpretation that reads like an extended metaphor. Nova Scotia is Canada's last best hope and a still relatively undiscovered place shaped by the sea. "Every state or province undoubtedly nurtures loyalty to its soil, "he writes, "but a land nearly surrounded by water and steeped in a history of the sea suggests kinship between the salt in the blood and the salt in the air."

(Above) Prolific writer Lesley Choyce, author of *Nova Scotia: Shaped by the Sea*.

Written as an odyssey of discovery by an American expatriate, Choyce waxes philosophical and succeeds in capturing the allure of Nova Scotia for those seeking refuge from the excesses and intrusions of contemporary North American society. "Historians often speak with some despair of the province as a place that has been out-of-step with major industrialized development and the inherent blessings that come along with that," he notes. "There is, for me, however, great comfort in in this thought that the world has passed us by. Now I can live here with fewer frills, fewer distractions, a limited amount of noise and observe the madness from a distance."

NOW OR NEVER NOVA SCOTIA

Five years ago, the Nova Scotia Commission on the New Economy, headed by then Acadia University president Ray Ivany, staked out a very different vision of the province's present and future. Released in February of 2014, the Ivany report entitled *Now or Never: An urgent call to action for Nova Scotians* identified disturbing economic and demographic trends and called upon Nova Scotian's to embrace entrepreneurship, harness immigration, and take charge of the province's future.

To most Nova Scotians, the Ivany report came as a cold shower, but whether it changed the province's trajectory is still being debated. One profoundly important comment, uttered by author John DeMont, seemed to capture the mood. "It's a great place here, there's no denying that. But it is hard slogging here. It has always been."

HISTORY, MEANING AND IDENTITY

Searching for turning points in Nova Scotia's history begins with identifying and assessing events of some historical significance. The province's entry into Confederation in the 1860s, flirtation with Secession in the 1880s, brush with Maritime Rights in the 1920s, and role in the two twentieth century world wars stand out as pivotal junctures in that history. What makes them "turning points" is that they represent an historical moment when a decisive change takes place affecting the province's destiny and place in the larger world. Scanning the historical landscape, it is possible to identify other equally pivotal points which signified longer-term social, cultural and economic changes. That is the very challenge tackled in this book.

Nova Scotia's history over the past 150 years has been played out along the "shifting axis" of Canadian east-west development. The older Scottish Canadian tradition of "tartanism" faded and Nova Scotian-ness found expression in different ways, in a more diverse, tolerant and accepting Maritime society and culture.

By the end of this volume, it is my hope that you will see the featured episodes as part of a bigger picture providing some fresh insights into where we are, where we've been, and where we're headed in the years ahead.

Digging Deeper – For Further Reading

Beck, J. Murray, ed., Joseph Howe: Voice of Nova Scotia. Toronto; McClelland & Stewart, 1964.

Careless, J.M.S., Frontier and Metropolis: Regions, Cities, and Identities in Canada before 1914. Toronto: University of Toronto Press, 1989.

Choyce. Lesley, Nova Scotia: Shaped by the Sea. Lawrencetown, NS: Pottersfield Press, 2005.

Conrad, Margaret and James K. Hiller, Atlantic Canada: A History. Toronto: Oxford University Press, 2015.

DeMont, John, The Long Way Home: A Personal History of Nova Scotia. Toronto: McClelland & Stewart, 2017.

Forbes, E.R., Challenging the Regional Stereotype: Essays on the 20th Century Maritimes. Fredericton, NB: Acadiensis Press, 1989.

McKay, Ian and Robin Bates, In the Province of History: The Making of the Public Past in Twentieth Century Nova Scotia. Montreal: McGill-Queen's University Press, 2010.

One Nova Scotia Commission, Now or Never: The Report of the Nova Scotia Commission on Building Our New Economy, Ray Ivany, Chair. Halifax: OneNS.ca, February 2014.

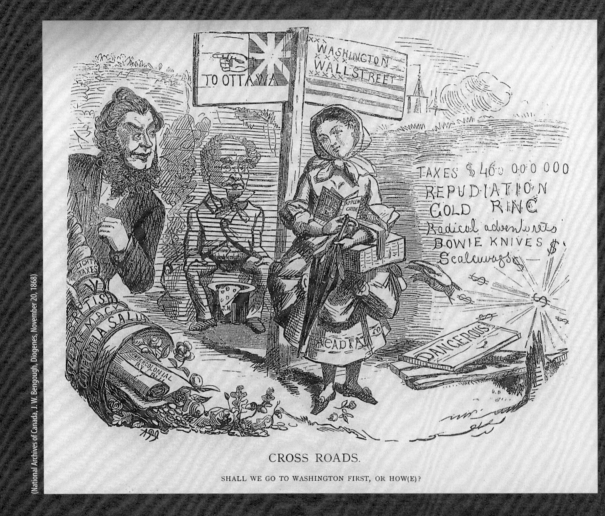

CROSS ROADS.

SHALL WE GO TO WASHINGTON FIRST, OR HOW(E)?

Turning Point 1

The Botheration Scheme:
Nova Scotia's Entry into Confederation, 1864-1870

Nova Scotia entered Confederation in 1867 as one of the four founding provinces, swallowing a federal union scheme shrouded in controversy. Premier Charles Tupper favoured Maritime Union and eventually embraced a broader union proposed by leading mainland Canadians like John A. Macdonald and Georges Etienne Cartier. The province's most recognizable public figure, Joseph Howe, labelled it a "Botheration Scheme" and fought to the end to block its passage.

One of Canada's leading historians, Dalhousie University's P. B. Waite, described well the birthing process 150 years ago. "Confederation was not, except in Canada West, what is usually referred to as a popular movement. It was imposed on British North America by ingenuity, luck, courage and sheer force." The federal union, he added, was achieved more through "political coalitions and colonial office dispatches."

The fierce debates over Confederation in Nova Scotia, pitting Dr. Charles Tupper against Joseph Howe, demonstrate that it was essentially a "Botheration Scheme" which refused to go away. The country doctor from Amherst, Cumberland County, popularly known as the "Bulldog of Confederation," remained undeterred and used every trick in the book of politics to overcome Howe and the Anti-Confederates or Antis.

The public debate over Confederation played out in a Nova Scotia near the zenith of its economic prosperity, yet facing a fundamental socio-economic transformation. With a population of some 350,000, the Atlantic colony was riding high in the golden age of wood, wind and sail. "Our province," the Morning Chronicle reported on December 18, 1865, was "prosperous beyond compare" and "on the full tide of prosperity under the lowest tariff in America."

Merchant shipping and shipbuilding drove the economy, but new elites were emerging committed to a new industrialism based upon railway building, development of the northern coalfields and nurturing an infant iron and steel industry. Spearheaded by Tupper, premier of Nova Scotia since May 1864, the industrial expansionists were decidedly pro-Confederation, while the traditional, more dominant mercantile class, centred in Halifax and larger port towns, resisted any change.

'QUEBEC RESOLUTIONS'

The federal union plan, hatched at the September 1864 Charlottetown Conference but later labelled the "Quebec Resolutions," was opposed by Howe and the Antis because it threatened the status quo and offered the uncertain promise of greater material progress. Although the Anti-Confederation League was slow to get organized, it was a formidable force backed by the merchant and shipping interests.

Maritime Union and, when it fell short, broader British North American Union, were bold political ideas championed first by Premier Tupper. "It was his idea," Tupper biographer Jock Murray recently pointed out, "and he deserves more recognition for this signal contribution."

That may be accurate, but — it must also be recognized — Confederation arose at a politically opportune time for the Premier. Introducing the first Schools Act in 1864 had made him unpopular. The school legislation, hailed today as the origin of Nova Scotia's public school system, had imposed a direct tax on Nova Scotians that tied provincial school grants to local assessments levied "voluntarily" by local school districts. Farsighted or not, it was fiercely resisted, particularly in rural districts where aggrieved citizens in four different villages burned their schools to the ground in local tax protests.

(Opposite) Five of Nova Scotia's Fathers of Confederation: Charles Tupper, Jonathan McCully, and Robert B. Dickey from Amherst and surrounding Cumberland County together with Adams G. Archibald of Truro and William A. Henry of Baddeck, Cape Breton .

Honble Charles Tupper,
Prov^l Secy., N.S.

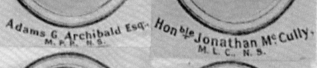

Adams G. Archibald Esqr.,
M.P.P., N.S.

Honble Jonathan Mc.Cully,
M.L.C., N.S.

Honble William A. Henry,
Attorney General, N.S.

Honble Robert B. Dickey,
M. Leg. Council, N.S.

(Chronicle Herald Archives)

In 1864 Tupper brought about the Conference at Charlottetown to discuss Confederation.

The Quebec Conference followed.

Howe opposed the Quebec scheme of Confederation.

Nonetheless, on

JULY 1, 1867

The British North America Act came into effect.

Howe, in failing health, entered the Canadian Cabinet of Sir John A. Macdonald and in May, 1873, was appointed Lieutenant-Governor of Nova Scotia.

JOSEPH HOWE... orator, newspaperman and statesman, died June 1, 1873, but his place in Nova Scotia's history will long be remembered.

DESIGNED AND PRODUCED BY COMIC BOOK WORLD, 2678 HIGH STREET, HALIFAX, NOVA SCOTIA

(Left) Special Edition of the *NovaScotian* glorifies "Nova Scotia's Joseph Howe" and gives very short shrift to Charles Tupper, the premier who brought the province into Confederation. In the Comic Book World version, Tupper's role in Confederation is essentially excluded, federal union is simply announced, and the tale ends with Howe's final honour – appointment as Lieutenant- Governor of Nova Scotia.

Proposing Confederation, P.B. Waite has contended, served Tupper's purpose by "diverting public attention from awkward issues of provincial politics." When Nova Scotians started rallying against the proposed union, the Premier remained absolutely resolute. Tagged by biographer Murray as the "Fighting Doctor," Tupper was, in the words of the Montreal *Gazette*, "forcible, keen and emphatic" and his determined face, curly back hair and mutton-chop side-whiskers conveyed the image of a pugnacious lion leading with his chin.

The Confederation plan surfaced while Nova Scotia's defender of the press and father of responsible government Joseph Howe was in a hiatus from active politics. After three years as Premier and 27 long years of public service, he had stepped down in 1863 determined to stay clear of the seemingly petty issues of local politics.

That all changed in January 1865 when the *Morning Chronicle's* proprietor, Charles Annand, sacked his pro-Confederate editor Jonathan McCully and the paper instantly became the leading opposition paper in Nova Scotia. One day after the announcement, January 11, 1865, the first of 12 successive "Botheration Letters" appeared, unsigned but authored by none other than Joseph Howe. They were unsigned because, at the time, Howe was serving as the Fisheries Commissioner, a senior public service post.

Tired and somewhat embittered, Howe was awakened by Confederation, which he found deeply disconcerting. While championing reciprocity in trade, he had grown less enamoured with the idea of British North American union. He came to view maintaining good relations with the British Empire as more important than joining in with "the Canadians."

'BOTHERATION LETTERS'

His antipathy toward Tupper — a brash, supremely confident politician whom he considered an "upstart doctor" from Cumberland on the provincial frontier — ran deep. "I will not play second fiddle to that d…. d Tupper," he reportedly quipped. The appearance of the "Botheration Letters" marked the formal breech and led to some of the fiercest and epic public debates ever to be witnessed in the province.

The Letters appeared as 12 lengthy editorials in the Halifax *Morning Chronicle* from January 11 to March 2, 1965. While the author was anonymous, the flair, eloquence and sarcastic wit were recognizable as Howe's unique style of writing. In the editorials, Howe essentially summed up all of the main arguments against Confederation.

His lively and engaging style breathed new life into the Antis and played upon the fears of Nova Scotians. Letter No. 2, on January 13, 1865, targeted federal union as the creation of French Canadians who, ever since the 1841 Union of Upper and Lower Canada, had acted as a bloc and controlled the united legislature. He predicted that the French Canadians in Canada East would "back their Local Legislature against the United Parliament." In the most vivid passage, he asked: "Was Sampson stronger when the false Delilah got him confederated, bound him up with cords and cut off his hair?"

Howe's letters appealed to Nova Scotian patriotism and rallied opponents in every corner of the province. From the bully pulpit of the *Morning Chronicle*, he exposed the control over the colonial press exercised by the Quebec delegates committed to federal union. First the independent *Halifax Citizen*, and now the *Morning Chronicle*, he claimed, were "shaking off old trammels." With the press speaking out, he concluded in the final March 2 letter, "the Botheration Scheme was ventilated in every part of the Province, and so far as Nova Scotia is concerned, may now be considered as dead as Julius Caesar."

Premier Tupper sought a broader union and was not inclined to let anything stand in his way. Below the surface, British colonial officials provided surprisingly astute insights into the collective identity and psyche of Nova Scotians.

(Library and Archives Canada)

(Top) "Nova Scotia's Joseph Howe in repose.

POLITICAL MANIPULATION

Lieutenant-Governor Richard MacDonnell (1864-1865), for example, advised Governor General Lord Monck early in 1865 that the Canadian office may not have correctly read the "Bluenose who is happy as he is. Your Ministry," he continued, "seem not to have suspected any rocks or shoals ahead while they were in reality trying to steer through a channel full of them." He went even further, calling into question "their political manipulation of the subject with so keen a spectator as Bluenose watching the game."

Tupper watched New Brunswick Premier Leonard Tilley suffer electoral defeat fighting for federal union and was determined to avoid an election on the Confederation issue he knew he could not win. Instead of calling an election on the Quebec Resolutions, he used his majority to pass them in the legislature. Lieutenant-Governor Sir William Fenwick Williams, the Nova Scotia-born

(Left) Dr. Charles Tupper, the Nova Scotia Premier who ushered the province into Canadian Confederation (Library andArchives Canada, PA-026318)

official who succeeded MacDonnell, acting upon directives from London, aided and abetted Tupper in removing potential legislative obstacles to federal union.

Rancour and divisiveness spilled over in public debates over the "Botheration Scheme." In the Shiretown of Pictou, a January 1865 Court House meeting exposed real division between the forces representing the "ayes" and "nays" and a resolution to delay legislative action until after the next general election resulted in a deadlock. Later in January 1865, fists flew in New Glasgow in what was described as a "temper-flaring breakup."

Tupper succeeded in fending-off the Antis. From July 1866 to May 1867, Howe led a delegation to England to oppose the passage of the act of union, only to be rebuffed, as the British North America Act confederating the four colonies passed without much debate or fanfare.

'ILLEGITIMATE' CHILD

Digging Deeper – For Further Reading

Beck, J. Murray, *Joseph Howe, Anti-Confederate*. Ottawa: The Canadian Historical Association, 1965.

Beck, J. Murray, *Joseph Howe, Vol. II, The Briton Becomes Canadian 1848-1873*. Halifax: Formac Publishing, 1984.

Bennett, Paul W., "Confederation and the Maritimes: Why Did Maritimers Respond with Such Ambivalence to the Idea of Federal Union?" in Bennett and Cornelius J. Jaenen, *Emerging Identities: Problems and Interpretations in Canadian History*. Scarborough: Prentice-Hall, 1986.

Murray, Jock and Janet, *Sir Charles Tupper: Fighting Doctor to Father of Confederation*. Markham: Fitzhenry & Whiteside, 1999.

Waite, Peter B., *The Life and Times of Confederation, 1864-1867: Politics, Newspapers and the Union of British North America*. Toronto: University of Toronto Press, 1962.

The first Dominion Day, July 1, 1867, demonstrated the depth of the divisions over Canadian Confederation. All over rural Pictou County, the news was greeted with silence. Some Confederate flags did appear, but so did flags flown upside down, at half mast or coloured black. No church bells were rung, no gun salutes were fired and no congratulations were offered. The headlined editorial in the New Glasgow *Eastern Chronicle* claimed that Nova Scotians are now "said to be Canadians against your wishes." One rural paper condemned federal union as "an Infant Monster of Confederation and a black day for Nova Scotians." Editorial death notices appeared, declaring the birth of an "illegitimate" child — the Dominion of Canada — and mourning the passing of "John Bluenose, aged 118 years."

Tupper and the Confederates may have ushered in the birth of the Dominion, but they suffered crushing defeat in the first provincial and federal elections held after federal union. In the Nova Scotia election of 1867, 36 of 38 seats were taken by the Anti-Confederates and in the ensuing federal election, Sir Charles Tupper was the only Confederate re-elected, in Cumberland, as 18 of 19 seats went to opponents of the union.

Pushing through Canadian Confederation was one of Tupper's most enduring legacies, but he paid a heavy price for ramming it through the legislature. A towering statue honouring Nova Scotia's leading Anti-Confederate graces the lawn of Province House, while our first Premier of the Confederation era remains unrecognized in the main provincial square.

Today, Joseph Howe is revered more for defending press freedoms and lighting the path to responsible government than for his divisive Anti-Confederation campaign. That's the upshot of J. Murray Beck's classic 1983 biography, *Joseph Howe: The Briton Becomes Canadian* 1848-1873. Unlike Tupper, he failed to see the potential of a British North American union in the 1860s. Few recall his visceral anti-French Canadianism, dating back to a May 1849 letter, rejecting joining a nation with "a helot and inferior race within its bosom." His Nova Scotia patriotism led him to grossly exaggerate the evils that would befall his native province under union. Nor did he recognize the total unacceptability of his own proposal for Nova Scotia in a reorganized British empire.

His description of Confederation as a "Botheration Scheme" has much less resonance today. As a brilliant orator, Howe's words pulled at the heartstrings of Nova Scotians: "Take a Nova Scotian to Ottawa, away above tidewater, freeze him up for five months, where he cannot view the Atlantic, smell salt water, or see the sail of a ship, and the man will pine and die." Nova Scotia's under-recognized Father of Confederation, Sir Charles Tupper, could never top his flair for capturing the identity and sensibilities of Nova Scotians.

Turning Point 2

Nova Scotia Secession:
Premier William Fielding's Forgotten Drive, 1886-1887

(Opposite) William S. Fielding: Dashing young reporter for the Halifax *Morning Chronicle*, William S. Fielding, future Premier of Nova Scotia, and campaigner for Repeal of the Confederation agreement. In 1873, he achieved some early notoriety for his coverage of the SS *Atlantic* disaster. A year later, he became Editor of The *Nova Scotian*, and Managing Editor of the *Morning Chronicle*, the province's most influential newspaper

Separatism is not unknown in the Nova Scotian political tradition. From March 1885 until February 1887, secession from Confederation was a live proposition, dominating newspaper coverage of provincial politics. At the centre of the mostly forgotten controversy was Nova Scotia Premier William S. Fielding, a former journalistic protégé of Joseph Howe at the *Morning Chronicle*, and a Nova Scotian still harbouring Anti-Confederate sentiments formed under Howe's tutelage in the mid-1860s.

After a series of failed attempts to redress Nova Scotia's grievances with Ottawa, the Liberal Government of Fielding won a popular mandate on June 15, 1886 to repeal the federal union agreement, winning 29 of the 38 seats in the Legislative Assembly. When the Fielding-led repeal campaign fizzled out in the subsequent federal election of 1887, secession ultimately disappeared.

The abortive secession movement should not be dismissed as one of a series of repeated Maritime regional protests or a minor blip in federal-provincial relations. It was, as Saint Mary's University historian Colin D. Howell once reminded us, a secession movement borne of the dire socioeconomic conditions affecting the Maritimes in the 1880s.

'REGIONAL IDEOLOGY'

Nova Scotian separatism was not simply a gambit concocted by Fielding and his allies to secure better terms from Ottawa. It grew out of what Howell termed a "regional ideology," which "attempted both to explain and to remedy the area's declining economic fortunes."

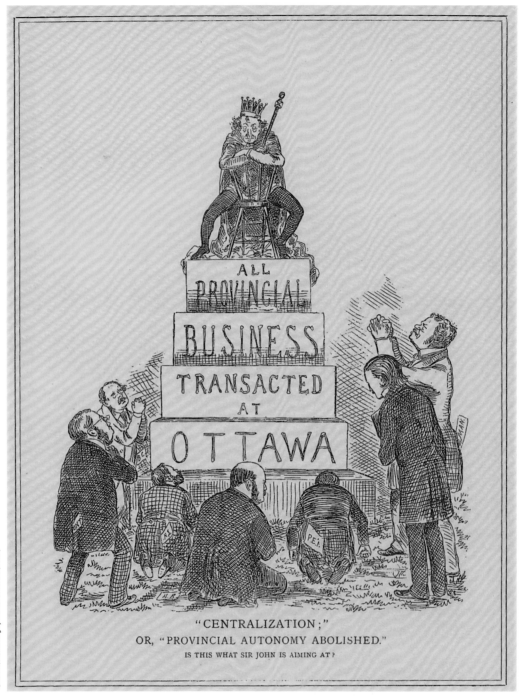

(Top) Centralization – or Provincial Autonomy Abolished: An 1882 political caricature by J.W. Bengough captured the worst fears of provincial premiers coming to terms with the Canadian federal system in the early 1880s. The king of the castle Sir John A. Macdonald favoured a more centralized 'legislative union' and one that contained the growth of provincial autonomy. In the case of Nova Scotia, it sowed the seeds for a movement to secede from the federation.

Nova Scotia secession was not a coherent body of thought, like Quebec sovereignty in the 1970s, but rather an amalgam of firmly held sentiments: a yearning for a return to a pre-Confederation 'golden age;' a conviction that federal union made economic conditions worse; a determination to renegotiate the financial terms of union; a belief that national tariff and railway policies were detrimental to the region; a feeling that closer commercial ties with the United States were desirable and a continued hope that Nova Scotia, and the Maritimes, would be better off going it alone.

Many Nova Scotians in the mid-1880s were deadly serious about seceding from Confederation and some were still holding out hope for a resurrection of Maritime Union. A leading proponent of secession, James A. Fraser, Liberal MLA for Guysborough, was far more vociferous than his party leader, Premier Fielding.

Dubbed by the *Halifax Morning Herald* as the "Abraham of the secessionists, their prophet and father," Fraser lamented a Confederation where "a loyal and contented people had been converted by act of parliament into a state of serfdom to Canadian greed and spoliation." His repeal resolutions, initially tabled March 12, 1885, fired up the secession movement but caught Fielding off guard, putting the Premier in an uncomfortable position.

In his reply to Fraser's resolutions, Fielding took care to leave all his options open. While he agreed with Fraser that Tupper's actions dragooning Nova Scotia into Confederation was "a political crime" and that, if it were possible to "obtain a release under fair conditions" then "the province would become happier and more prosperous than it is." Having conceded that, Fielding proposed a compromise. If, after a further round of discussions, the federal government took no steps to better Nova Scotia's position, then the Assembly would be forced to initiate a process leading to the severance of the political tie with Canada. That proposition carried by a vote of 20 to 13 and formed the basis of Liberal policy on repeal.

Fielding was conscious, as his biographer C. Bruce Fergusson phrased it, of the responsibility of carrying "the mantle of Howe." Since being hired in 1864, at age 16, as a journalist with the *Morning Chronicle*, he had fought Howe's battles in the paper's editorial pages and then rose through the ranks to become managing editor of the paper, where his name appeared as editor on the front page of *The Nova Scotian* from 1874 to 1884.

While heavily influenced by Howe's telling critique of Confederation, Fielding was a far more balanced and tactically sound politician. In spite of his Anti-Confederate sentiments, he was a pragmatist who, when pushed, refused to rule out the possibility that "better terms" could be worked out with the Dominion Government, enabling him to "view union with Canada with favour."

Resisting pressure from more radical Nova Scotia repealers, he continued to stand by his federal leader, Edward Blake, holding out hope for "some measure of relief" should the Liberals defeat John A. Macdonald and his Conservative government. "It is wise," he said, "to see that we do not, by being too precipitate, embarrass ourselves in our negotiations with the Dominion Government for better terms…" If that proved futile, he indicated he was prepared to "take into consideration whether it is advisable to seek a separation from the Dominion."

(Left) Down with Confederation! : A broadsheet from the Repeal Campaign in Lunenburg County in June 1886. Two successful Liberal candidates, Charles Edward Church and George Angus Ross, appeal to electors to reject Confederation in favour of Nova Scotia secession.

(NSARM, Quebec Interprovincial Conference, October 26, 1887, Photography Collection #11)

MARITIME UNION APPEAL

Following the initial repeal-resolution debate, Fielding did his best to promote Maritime Union apart from Canada. In June and July 1885, he visited Charlottetown to enlist the support of "leading men" and took the pulse of the province. He found the New Brunswick government of Andrew G. Blair to be timid on Maritime Union and detected little interest from the decidedly Conservative PEI government of W. W. Sullivan. "While there is some dissatisfaction, "Fielding concluded, "they are not prepared to join the movement." It was becoming, as political scientist J. Murray Beck showed in his revealing 1969 study, a venture fraught with frustration.

Fielding's old newspaper, the *Morning Chronicle*, was deeply disappointed at the response of neighbouring Maritime provinces. "Why do not the New Brunswickers show so much of a spirit of resentment (as the Nova Scotians)?" the paper asked in a late March 1885 editorial. "They are our fellow sufferers. An independent union of the lower provinces would be a most happy one. …Very moderate taxation would suffice to meet the real wants of the country as then constituted. There would be no big company like the (Canadian) Pacific (Railway), mopping up our money, and not squeezing the mop out save to float a palace, or new stock jobbing raid."

Secession and with it Maritime Union were resurrected in February 1886 when, at long last, John A. Macdonald's government in Ottawa flatly rejected Nova Scotia's plea for "better terms" of union. A Nova Scotia Assembly Committee was quickly convened and a second, more insistent request was forwarded to Ottawa.

(Opposite) Provincial Rights Advocate: William S. Fielding, Editor of The *Nova Scotian* 1974-1884, before he became Premier of Nova Scotia.

In the absence of any substantive reply, Fielding waved his initial objections in May 8, 1886 and moved a series of his own repeal resolutions. The new version was not appreciably different from what was first proposed by Fraser. The Assembly added a provision committing the government to put the question of repeal before the people in the next election.

Speaking in the Assembly in May 1886, the Premier called for significant change and came out squarely in favour of repeal: "We say we want repeal with a union of the Maritime Provinces. We cannot speak for them, of course. We say further, if we cannot get a union with them, we want repeal pure and simple."

THE REPEALERS

Two weeks after passing the repeal resolutions, the Premier called an election for June 15, 1886 on the question of secession. Fielding's abrupt conversion to outright separation sparked speculation about his real commitment to the cause. Prominent critics claimed that it smacked of blackmail to get Ottawa to agree to better terms. Seasoned political observers saw it as a strategy to maintain unity in the Nova Scotia Liberal Party by appeasing Fraser and the most adamant repealers.

When Fielding and the Liberals won 29 of the 38 seats in the Assembly, the leading newspapers interpreted the vote as a mandate to seek Maritime Union, or — short of that — Nova Scotia secession from Confederation. On June 17, 1886, the *Morning Chronicle* was effusive in its response, claiming that "should the matter be fairly placed before the people of New Brunswick and Prince Edward Island they would see it in the same light as do the people of Nova Scotia."

Fielding put on a brave front, knowing that Maritime Union had gained little traction, even though he did not concede that openly until some months later. On PE I, Sullivan's government was returned on June 30, 1886, and Fielding's appeals reportedly met with what the *Toronto Mail* described as "no enthusiastic response." New Brunswick Premier A.G. Blair advised him directly that he had no intention of submitting the Maritime Union proposal to his people or to the Legislature.

Premier Fielding was left with only one remaining option by September of 1886 — securing repeal by itself. With a federal election in the offing, he told a federal Liberal nominating convention in November 1886 that, to have any reasonable chance of success, the party must "remove the barrier to repeal" by electing a majority of candidates committed to taking Nova Scotia out of Confederation.

Fielding's federal Liberal allies were facing long odds in a campaign being waged against Macdonald's ruling Conservatives. The Prime Minister summoned former Premier Charles Tupper from London to oversee the Conservative campaign in Nova Scotia. While Fielding promoted repeal in his campaign speeches, he found some of the Liberal candidates, particularly in industrializing areas of the province, reluctant to speak in its favour. Supporting Liberal Leader Edward Blake, a man who had spoken publicly against secession, also hurt the cause. The February 22, 1887 federal election dealt Premier Fielding's repeal aspirations a death blow. While the Liberals polled two percent more votes than in the 1882 election, they won only seven of the 21 seats, unchanged from the previous election.

For Fielding, the federal election results were a bitter disappointment and dashed all hopes of repeal. Nova Scotians, he said, had lost "a glorious opportunity" and, unless they were "prepared to take the question up with greater firmness," the repeal movement would have "no reasonable hope of success."

'A FAILED EXPERIMENT'

When Premier Fielding suspended the repeal campaign on April 21, 1887, the leading critics had a field day picking apart the failed movement. The *Halifax Herald*, predecessor of the current paper, had the last word, announcing that "the legislature of Nova Scotia consigned the repeal jackass to the silent tomb." It also forecast that repeal would likely be replaced by "some other donkey with a different name, mayhap 'Commercial Union.'"

That prediction turned out to be rather prophetic. With the suspension of the repeal campaign, Fielding and the Liberals reverted to the more conventional policy of promoting reciprocity in trade (or commercial union) with the United States, attracting outside investment for the coal industry and embracing a broader movement for provincial rights. Fielding's adroit political skills enabled him to survive as Premier and he went on to serve as Canada's Minister of Finance from 1896 to 1911.

Repeal of Confederation slowly lost its appeal for Nova Scotians. A new industrial order was springing up in Nova Scotia and the Maritimes, spurred by the Conservatives' National Policy of tariff protection, further eroding the traditional Maritime wood, wind and sail economy and with it the basis of the Nova Scotia Anti-Confederate secession movement.

Digging Deeper – For Further Reading

Beck, J. Murray, The History of Maritime Union: A Study in Frustration. Fredericton: Commission on the Union of the Maritime Provinces, 1969.

Fergusson, C. Bruce, Hon. W.S. Fielding: Volume 1: The Mantle of Howe. Windsor, NS: Lancelot Press, 1970.

Fingard, Judith, "The 1880s: Paradoxes of Progress," in E.R. Forbes and D.A. Muise, eds., The Atlantic Provinces in Confederation. Toronto and Fredericton: University of Toronto Press, Acadiensis Press, 1993.

Howell, Colin D., "W.S. Fielding and the Repeal Elections of 1886 and 1887 in Nova Scotia," Acadiensis, Vol. VIII (Spring, 1979), pp. 28- 46.

TROOPS EMBARKING AT HALIFAX N.S.

Turning Point 3

Wartime Imperial Outpost:
Halifax at War, 1914-1918

(Opposite) Postcard Picture: Troops Embarking at Halifax, 1915.

Disaster history is dramatic, flashy, gory and easy to remember. The made-for-television 1992 *Heritage Minute* on the Halifax Explosion is a perfect example of the phenomenon. Far less known is the pivotal role Halifax and Nova Scotia played in waging what was known at the time as the Great War or the War to End All Wars and remembered today as the First World War.

Potted-plant history has a way of grabbing your attention. When Canadians were polled by the Dominion Institute in the 1990s, the Halifax Explosion topped the list of best known Canadian historical events. Ten years later, it still ranked as the best known of the 60 original Minutes, a true testament to the power of the vignette featuring telegraph operator Vince Coleman.

The surviving Canadian war dairies provide a far more comprehensive and deeper insight into what Halifax and Nova Scotia were really like during the Great War. Pouring over the diaries and letters of soldiers and nurses, a more comprehensive and deeper picture emerges of life and society in a British imperial outpost that functioned as the Atlantic gateway to the Western Front.

Two diaries recently resurrected by historian Brian Tennyson, formerly of Cape Breton University, provide rich, first-hand accounts of life in Halifax, on troop ships and at the front. The first edited diary, *Percy Willmot: A Cape Bretoner at War*, drew attention to the critical role played by Nova Scotians as part of the Canadian Expeditionary Force (CEF) in the Great War, and Tennyson followed up in 2013 with *Merry Hell: The Story of the 25th Battalion (Nova Scotia Regiment*, bringing back to life the recollections of one soldier, Robert N. Clements.

Much can also be learned from the war experiences of Nova Scotia-born nurses serving at the front. Among those travelling with the Canadian troops in the autumn of 1914 was Pictou County's Margaret MacDonald, the matron in charge of 101 volunteer nurses who were the first women to become full-fledged members of the CEF.

CANADA AT WAR

Canada was an undeniably British nation in August 1914 and, because Britain was at war, so was the Dominion of Canada. Sir Robert Laird Borden, a Halifax lawyer of the Conservative stripe trained at Dalhousie University, was the Prime Minister. Support for the war was so widespread that the Liberal Opposition leader from French-speaking Quebec, Wilfrid Laurier, was quick to endorse the war effort and to recognize that Canada must share in the burden of defending the British Empire.

Public enthusiasm for the Great War ran deep in Halifax and across Nova Scotia in the autumn of 1914. The declaration of war touched off recruiting drives that provided the first infusion of troops in a military campaign that was initially to be waged entirely by voluntary enlistment. Eleven infantry battalions were raised in Nova Scotia and, of those, two (the 25th Battalion and the 85th Battalion) saw action as distinct fighting units on the Western front in France and Belgium.

The first of the two Nova Scotia battalions to see action was the 25th Battalion (Nova Scotia Rifles), dubbed the "Mackenzie Battalion." Officially authorized on November 7, 1914, the battalion served in France and Belgium as part of the 5th Infantry Brigade, 2nd Canadian Division, from September 16, 2014 until the end of the war.

(Top) Officers of the 25th (Mackenzie) Battalion: Mackenzie Livingstone and Major Guy MacLean.

The Halifax Armories served as the Regiment's headquarters and recruitment offices were established in Sydney, Amherst, New Glasgow, Truro and Yarmouth. Of the 1,000 Nova Scotians that started with the battalion, after the first year of fighting, some 900 were killed, taken prisoner, injured or went missing. For those who fell on the mud-infested battle field, it proved to be "bloody hell" rather than "merry hell."

Attrition rates for the 25th Battalion were extraordinarily high because they represented the first wave of shock troops. Comparative data presented in Colonel G.W. L. Nicholson's official history of the CE.F show that, overall, fatal Canadian casualties of 60,661 represented just over nine percent of those who enlisted. That's much higher than the 41,992 lost in the Second World War, reported as just under four percent of total enlistment.

THE GREAT WAR PROJECT

War diary reports published as part of the 2014 Canadian Great War Project fill in the gaps in the story and are starkly revealing. Lieutenant-Colonel George Augustus Le Cain, of Round Hill, Annapolis County, a 52-year-old reservist, was appointed the first commander in recognition for his energetic recruitment efforts.

Recruits began arriving from all over the province in early November 2014, the battalion was organized into eight different companies and, a month later, some 1,100 men had answered the call. Surviving photos show the 25th Battalion drilling in the fog on the Halifax Common and marching on Brunswick Street in a church parade. On December 17, 2014, Prime Minister and the Minister of Militia Major-General Sam Hughes reviewed the assembled troops and rallied them with patriotic speeches.

Massing the troops in the Armouries caused overcrowding and the spread of infectious diseases, particularly diphtheria. Some 350 soldiers-in-training were dispatched to the Immigration Building to relieve the overcrowding. In early February 2015, some 100 more recruits were enlisted to replace those discharged as "medically unfit and undesirable."

The big day for Nova Scotia recruits was May 20, 2015, when the troops embarked on the HMTS *Saxonia* after a parade march through the city of Halifax. Thousands of people crowded the streets to see the battalions board the ship. The 22nd Battalion of mostly French Canadians (today known as the 'Van Doos' or Vingt-Deux), arrived from Amherst at 3:00 pm and the Saxonian set sail three hours later.

The troop ship, fully loaded with 2,274 officers and men and packing a cache of weapons and ammunition, took nine days to reach Plymouth, England. The hastily-trained CEF boys were dispatched to various British training camps, and the 25th Battalion travelled by train to East Sandling Camp, Shorncliffe.

(Top) Robert L. Borden of Halifax, Prime Minister during the Great War 1914-1918.

Lieut Col. LeCain.
25th Battalion

(Left) First Commanding Officer, 25th Battalion, Nova Scotia Rifles, Lieut. Colonel George Augustus Le Cain, Round Hill, Annapolis Valley.

NIGHT OPERATIONS

Considered raw and lightly trained, they were drilled for three and a half more months, eight hours a day with regular four-hour "night operations" exercises. Their Canadian-made boots wore out and had to be replaced by British standard issue, known as "Lord Kitchener's boots."

Finally, on September 15, 2015, no less than 10 months after they began training, the 5th Brigade travelled from Folkstone to Boulogne, France, then by train from Port de Brieques to St. Omer, France. They reached the front lines in Belgium after a five-day march in their new boots. The Nova Scotian Mackenzie Battalion took up combat positions near Ypres, Belgium, and on September 22-23, 2015, became the first Nova Scotians to see action in the war.

The Nova Scotia 25th Battalion saw combat action in the war's worst theatre of conflict, spending 164 of its first 339 days on frontline duty in the dangerous and rain-soaked Belgian trenches. Members of the battalion, reinforced by recruits, were on the ground in most of the infamous battles, including Hill 62, the Somme, Flers-Courcelette, Ancre Heights, Vimy Ridge, and Passchendaele. Of the 5,120 soldiers who served, 718 (or 14 percent) died on the battlefield and 2,713 (or 53 percent) were wounded in action.

The First World War was not entirely a man's war at the front. Some 300 women from the Maritimes went overseas as nurses. One of the most notable was New Glasgow-born Charlotte "Lottie" Urquhart, who trained to be a nursing sister at Laval Hospital in Quebec City. Her enlistment papers, now posted prominently on the Library and Archives Canada website, stand out because she was a woman, assigned to the Medical Corps and from Nova Scotia.

(Right) Canadian Garrison Artillery, Detachment No. 4 Company, drilling at Fort Charlotte, Halifax, 1914.

(NSARM/ NovaScotia Archives)

(Left) Nova Scotia's 25th Battalion assembled in front of Halifax Armouries, 1914.

(British Library Collection)

Lottie Urquhart enlisted as a nurse in Montreal and, by September 1918, she was working at the No. 6 Canadian General Field Hospital at Point-le-Pont, near Paris. That hospital was directly hit on September 16, 1918 by one of the final German air raids of the war. Despite bombs falling on her ward, Urquhart continued to attend to the wounded. For that display of courage she was one of only six Canadian nurses awarded the Military Medal.

ON THE HOME FRONT

The mass exodus of enlistment-age men and the wartime carnage also created new opportunities for women to shore up the home front and take on new and unfamiliar roles. Nova Scotian enlistees shivering in the Halifax Armouries in late December 1915 were appreciative of the Halifax and Dartmouth Red Cross Societies' welcome gifts, 1,000 pairs of wristlets and 900 mufflers. After the Halifax Explosion, women carried the heaviest burden of home rebuilding and a dozen women stepped in as streetcar conductors to operate the city's tram cars.

Prominent Canadian imperial nationalists led by Prime Minister Borden saw Halifax on the front line in the defence of the British Empire. The Great War was, in Borden's eyes, virtually a British holy war to save threatened values — freedom, democracy, the rule of law and respect for human dignity. While this imperial vision was rather skewed, it did form the core of Borden's appeal to Nova Scotians and the broad Canadian populace. When the war worsened in early 1917 and casualties far exceeded new reinforcements, the Prime Minister broke his pledge and enacted conscription for overseas service.

Borden's home, Halifax, figured prominently in his speeches in defense of the conscription of men to fight on the Western Front. In the 1917 debate on the Conscription bill, he claimed that while the front line was in France and Flanders Field the Dominion was a transatlantic projection of British and European civilization.

"When the Canadians on the 22nd day of April 1915 barred the path of the Germans to Calais," Borden declared, "I say that they barred his path also to Halifax, Quebec, Saint John and Montreal." It was clear that Halifax was on "Canada's first line of defence" against the "horrors and barbarities" perpetrated by the German forces. "What security is there in mere distance?"

he asked, considering advances modern communications and weaponry on land, sea and air. His punchline: "Let us not forget that German submarines crossed the Atlantic nearly a year ago."

Today we tend to forget how threatened Halifax and likely most Nova Scotians were by the First World War. From October 1914 onward, Halifax swelled with fresh recruits and served as the most important gateway and metaphoric bridge to the war raging in Belgium and France. An estimated 350,000 Canadian men and women boarded ships to be taken overseas — and 60,000 never returned home.

The Last Steps Memorial Arch, located on the Halifax pier near the Maritime Museum of the Atlantic and unveiled in August 2016, bears silent witness to the critical role Nova Scotia's largest port city played in sending Canadian soldiers off to war. That memorial was inspired by Halifax Citadel Army Museum curator Ken Hynes and volunteer Museum governor Corrine MacLellan. Since the Halifax waterfront was where the departing soldiers took their last steps, the "footprints" of actual First World War army boots have been installed right next to the arch. It's a fitting reminder of a time when Halifax was at the crossroads of the Canadian nation.

Digging Deeper - for Further Reading

Conrad, Margaret R. and James K. Hillier, Atlantic Canada: A Concise History. Don Mills, ON: Oxford University Press, 2006.

Clements, Robert N., Merry Hell: The Story of the 25th Battalion (Nova Scotia Regiment), Canadian Expeditionary Force 1914-1919. Edited by Brian Tennyson. Toronto: University of Toronto Press, 2013.

Hunt, M. Stuart, Nova Scotia's Part in the Great War. Halifax: Nova Scotia Veterans Publishing Company, 1920.

Nicholson, Col. G. W. L., Canadian Expeditionary Force, 1914-1919: Official History of the Canadian Army in the First World War. Originally published 1962. Montreal and Kingston: McGill-Queen's University Press, 2015.

Tennyson, Brian D., Nova Scotia at War, 1914-1919. Halifax: Nimbus, 2017.

Tennyson, Brian D., Percy Willmot: Cape Bretoner at War. Sydney: Cape Breton University Press, 2007.

Turning Point 4

Maritime Rights:
The Rise and Fall of the Movement, 1919-1927

A small pamphlet produced on September 15, 1924 and entitled *Nova Scotia's Right to Live* demonstrated that Nova Scotia's problems with Confederation were far from resolution. Written by a well-heeled Halifax financier, F. B. McCurdy, the tract made a stirring case for Nova Scotia to claim its "fair share of the commonwealth." Alarmed by a westward shift in the axis of Confederation and frustrated by a federation extracting "tribute to Ontario and Quebec," he suggested that Nova Scotians again consider secession as a remedy of last resort.

That pamphlet embodied the most radical expression of "Maritime Rights," a regional protest movement, which surfaced in Nova Scotia and her neighbouring provinces in the years after the First World War. Unlike the Prairie West, where post-war protest produced new political parties, the regional discontent was channeled through the traditional party system, championed by the federal and regional Conservative politicians, and lacked the staying power of third-party movements.

Nova Scotia's Maritime Rights agitation sprang from deep-seated grievances festering since the time of Confederation. Discontent voiced in the 1920s was a manifestation of both the Maritimes regional economic decline and its loss of political clout in the federal Parliament in Ottawa. Prime Minister Mackenzie King and his "solid sixteen" Liberal members of Parliament, elected in 1920 and including former Nova Scotia champion William S. Fielding, bore the brunt of the growing eastern resistance.

(Donald McRitchie Fonds, Acadia University Archives)

(Left) Room for More Rights: *Halifax Herald* cartoonist Donald McRitchie depicts the Maritime Club of Halifax being summoned in 1924 to board the train to prosperity for the region. The Moncton, Saint John, and Truro club members are already on board that train, likely headed to Ottawa.

'MARITIME RIGHTS'

Signs of agrarian and labour dissent were present in Nova Scotia, but the late Ernest R. Forbes seminal 1979 book, *Maritime Rights*, demonstrated that the movement gave expression to a broader consensus that Nova Scotia and the Maritimes were an after-thought whose concerns did not register in Ottawa.

As the leading voice for Maritime Rights, the *Halifax Herald* under publisher William H. Dennis, surpassed the *Morning Chronicle* in readership and threw its considerable editorial weight behind the Conservatives. It was a time when newspaper editorials moved votes in the province.

The Maritime Rights movement of the 1920s challenges, in many ways, the prevailing stereotype of Maritime conservatism and resistance to change. Examining the roots of the agitation reveals that it was much more than a tempest in a teapot stirred up by Nova Scotia elites and their captive politicians. It was, in other words, a regional protest fired by broader, deeper discontent.

The organized delegations to Ottawa, board of trade conferences, countrywide speaking tours and stinging editorials attracted most of the press attention. Prominent businessmen did most of the talking, political party support shifted dramatically and the beleaguered King Liberals finally responded with a royal commission. University of New Brunswick professor Forbes, the de-facto dean of Atlantic Studies, put it all in perspective: "There was far more to 'Maritime Rights,'" he once stated, "than the conspicuous wail of the politicians."

A severe post-war recession hit a number of Maritime industries hard. Declines in export prices for lumber and fish, higher American tariffs and domestic freight rates, the end of the wartime construction boom, shrinking farm income and branch plant closures all hurt employment levels, spelling economic trouble. Declining post-war demand for iron and steel and the impact of a 1920 consolidation that created the British Empire Steel Corporation (BESCO), resulted in a loss of Cape Breton control, the slashing of wages and deteriorating labour-management relations.

(Right) Real Encouragement: Maritime Rights advocates waving the flag of unity head to Ottawa, 1925. One of a series of Donald McRitchie cartoons that accompanied the increasingly strident *Halifax Herald* editorials promoting the cause.

(Halifax Herald, 3 October 1925)

Real Encouragement

(Halifax Herald, 18 April 1915)

THAT'S THE SPIRIT

(Left) That's The Spirit: Nova Scotia is depicted as a small boy seeking its "fair share" out of the federal-provincial pie, 1925. The Canadian host in a Mountie hat carves up the pie representing shares of Canadian trade. The book on the table indicates he's playing "The Game of Canadian Unity" by pitting one province against another.

The Port of Halifax's share of Canadian shipping activity fell from 20.3 percent in 1919 to only 8.5 percent seven years later. Central Canadian railways, most notably Canadian National, not only levied higher freight rates on Maritime producers, but they also favoured shipping to export markets through the Atlantic Terminal of the former Grand Trunk Railway in Portland, Maine.

Consolidating railways was bad for the Maritimes and it culminated in 1923 with the formation of the Canadian National Railway system and the advent of a new management neither sympathetic nor knowledgeable about Maritime concerns. In a fateful and determined effort to standardize freight rates, which Professor Forbes labelled a policy of "misguided symmetry," the national Board of Railway Commissioners increased freight rates on the CNR line east of Montreal to the level of those in Central Canada. This adjustment fell unevenly on resource-producing provinces with cargoes generally heavier in weight. The national railway became what historian George Rawlyk aptly described as "the *bete-noir* of the Maritimes" and "the single most important source of anti-Ottawa animus."

LOSING INFLUENCE

The Maritimes was losing influence in Ottawa, where representation in Parliament tended to reflect changes in the region's relative population. The number of Maritime seats in the House of Commons declined from 43 seats in the 1870s to 31 in 1921. In the case of Nova Scotia, representation dropped from 21 to 16 seats. During that time, the Maritimes lost further ground because the size of the House of Commons actually increased from 206 seats in 1874 to 235 in 1921. Before the 1925 election, Nova Scotia lost two more seats, even though the House expanded by 10 seats.

Prime Minister King was a master political tactician and, for a time, he successfully wooed the Maritimes. After succeeding Sir Wilfrid Laurier in 1919, King entered the House as a Liberal member for Prince County, Prince Edward Island, and showed initial sympathy for regional causes. In the 1921 federal election, the Maritimes elected Liberals in 25 of the 31 seats and King secured a minority government, sustained by brokering alliances with a new crop of Western Progressives. One of the most powerful cabinet members, former Nova Scotia premier W.S. Fielding, had left Nova Scotia to live in Ottawa and no longer identified himself with regional interests.

Making political concessions to the Western Progressives kept King in office in the early 1920s. His most telling move came in 1922, when King renewed the contested Crownest Pass freight-rate structure, heavily favouring the interests of Western Canadian grain growers. Doing so while ignoring Maritimers' objections to a 40 percent hike in rates for the Intercolonial Railway, which served Nova Scotia, New Brunswick, Quebec and Ontario, only compounded the growing eastern alienation from the Liberal government in Ottawa.

Outspoken Conservatives found a champion in McCurdy, a former cabinet minister with strong views of his own. In a September 1923 personal letter to Conservative leader Arthur Meighan, he impressed upon the leader the urgency of the province's plight.

"Economically … Nova Scotia is bleeding to death," McCurdy stated. Turning down an invitation to run for the Conservatives in Halifax, he also expressed concern over the federal party's policies. "I am satisfied," he wrote, "that anyone who embarks on politics without a remedy for existing ills will only be serving an exasperated public and will enjoy a very brief tenure of office — not worth the effort."

A FISCAL STRAITJACKET

From 1924 to 1925, McCurdy sharpened his critique of the fiscal policy of Canada. Federalism had become a fiscal straitjacket for Nova Scotia, he contended, where the so-called National Policy failed to recognize or protect either Maritime interests or its ocean ports. What the Maritimes needed, he concluded, was "an opportunity to live our own lives … under fiscal arrangements that are suitable to our needs." He saw the Nova Scotia government rather than either of the federal parties as the best means of addressing the problems.

(Library and Archives Canada)

(Top) Masterful Politician: William Lyon Mackenzie King, Prime Minister and dominant political leader throughout the 1920s who held office for almost 22 years.

Frustration in Parliament spilled over and fired up the Maritime Board of Trade and related groups to go public with a Maritime Rights campaign aimed at educating the public, in the provinces and across the country, about the legitimate concerns of Maritimers. Initially conceived as a broad non-partisan initiative, the campaign sought to mobilize local business groups and to extend its influence through a "national appeal" to enlist support for Maritime grievances.

Local boards of trade were the most prominent supporters of Maritime Rights and they sponsored meetings on regional issues and organized trainloads of delegates to carry the message to Ottawa. With King's Liberals occupied wooing the Western Progressives, the "traditional social and political elite" of the region gravitated to the only political alternative, Meighan and his Conservative Party.

Gradually, the whole movement was appropriated by the Conservatives, especially in Nova Scotia. Publishers of the most prominent Conservative newspapers, spearheaded by Dennis of the *Halifax Herald*, with the energetic support of Harris Sinclair (H.S.) Congdon, a former high school principal and Dartmouth journalist, effectively and relentlessly promoted the cause.

Herald publisher Dennis viewed McCurdy's agitation as a "diabolical" internal conspiracy that threatened to tear the Conservative Party apart over the question of secession. The Nova Scotia Liberals' sudden shift in early 1925 to support Maritime Rights only added to the Dennis faction's fears and suspicions about the McCurdy insurgency.

When the provincial Liberals endorsed a thinly veiled version of McCurdy's Maritime Rights policy in April 1925, Dennis and his supporters saw the transformation as further evidence of disloyalty. Coupled with McCurdy's close relationship by marriage to the owner of the rival *Morning Chronicle*, Dennis ally Congdon concluded that McCurdy had "gone over to the Liberals."

The fierce competitiveness of Dennis and the editorial consistency of the *Halifax Herald* paid dividends in the newspaper wars. Steadfast support for Maritime Rights, coupled with a bid for labour support, won the *Herald* new subscribers in the 1920s. An independent audit released in 1926 by Dennis revealed a net gain of 75 percent in subscriptions for the *Herald* and the *Mail* between 1921 and 1926. The new readers came at the expense of the once dominant *Morning Chronicle*, a paper facing such serious economic woes that it had to be bailed out in 1925 by the Liberal Party.

THE ELECTORAL COLLAPSE

The Conservatives' revival in the Maritimes was propelled by its advocacy of Maritime Rights. It began with a by-election victory by Conservative W.A. Black in Halifax in 1923. In the ensuing 1925 Nova Scotia election, the Conservatives under newly-installed leader E.N. Rhodes swept 40 of the 43 seats in the Legislature, capturing a record 60.9 percent of the popular vote. Federal Conservative leader Meighen reaped the benefits in the 1925 federal election, where King Liberals were punished for ignoring Nova Scotia grievances, and 23 of the province's 29 seats ended up in the Conservative column.

**Digging Deeper –
for Further Reading**

Forbes, Ernest R., Maritime Rights: The Maritime Rights Movement, 1919-1927: A Study in Regionalism. Montreal: McGill-Queen's University Press, 1979.

Frank, David, "The 1920s: Class and Region, Resistance and Accommodation," in E. R. Forbes and D.A. Muise, eds., The Atlantic Provinces in Confederation. Toronto and Fredericton: University of Toronto Press/Acadiensis Press, 1993.

March, William, Red Line: The Chronicle-Herald and The Mail-Star. Halifax: Chebucto Agencies Limited, 1986.

Rawlyk, George, The Atlantic Provinces and the Problems of Confederation. St. John's, NL: Breakwater Books, 1979.

Stunned by the Maritime electoral collapse, Prime Minister King finally decided to act in response to the Maritime Rights movement. He responded in typical King fashion, shovelling the problem off to a Royal Commission. The Commission, under the leadership of Sir Andrew Rae Duncan, exceeded most expectations. It encouraged a full hearing of the region's grievances and produced a practical and implementable report in 1926.

The Duncan Commission report paid due respect to the region's historic grievances, but argued that it was not possible to right the wrongs committed since federal union in 1867. It did, however, propose some practical solutions to the difficult problems, demonstrating the legitimacy of Maritime grievances to politicians and citizens in the rest of Canada.

The Nova Scotia press was generally euphoric in its response to the Duncan report. Most took their cue from W.H. Dennis of the Herald, where the lead editorial described the report as the "Maritime Magna Carta." The Commission recommended a revision and increase in provincial subsidies, favourable changes in railway rate structures, regional flexibility in setting freight rates, subsidies for coke plants and the creation of harbour commissions in Halifax and Saint John.

APPEASEMENT POLICY

Prime Minister King played his political cards most effectively. In spite of leaked cabinet documents outlining what critics labelled an "appeasement policy," he publicly insisted that his Liberal government was committed to acting upon the report. Maritime newspapers, including the Herald and Mail, like others across the nation, were prepared to accept the Prime Minister's assurances that the recommendations were being implemented "virtually in their entirety."

Amidst the flurry of overblown praise and premature self-congratulation, the Maritime Rights movement simply faded away. A few board of trade representatives maintained what George Rawlyk described as "a lonely vigil to ensure that the government followed through on its promises." Without the public pressure exerted by a vocal movement, federal policymakers of both major parties reverted to playing the game that Mackenzie King had perfected, brokerage politics playing one regional interest against another.

Relying upon King to honour commitments may have been unwise. A sage political observer, Frank R. Scott, read the Prime Minister better than most. King plucked off a few recommendations and then turned the balance of the measures over to board committees and further studies, causing delays and debates, all tending to "diffuse" the regional protest movement. As Scott's famous 1957 poem, "W.L.M.K.," showed, King had piled a "Parliamentary Committee on a Royal Commission … to … postpone, postpone …." It was sleight of hand because, in Scott's words, his "one hand" knew "what the other was doing."

Even the federal Conservatives, the most outspoken champions of the movement, proved themselves to be "Conservatives first and Maritimes Righters second." In the absence of a broad non-partisan campaign or a regional protest party, the movement lost steam and credibility. "The ritualistic shibboleths of Maritime Rights," Rawlyk aptly observed, "made for good political rhetoric" and, while they did "help win elections," could be "put away until the next election."

Turning Point 5

The Bluenose Legacy:
Fame, Commemoration and Identity, 1929-1937

A fishing and racing schooner is the most instantly recognizable public symbol of Nova Scotia. The *Bluenose*, it seems, is almost everywhere — from the Canadian dime to our license plates and from a beer label to tourist souvenirs. It remains as ubiquitous in Nova Scotia as the light-houses on our shores, Sobeys in our towns and cities and Tim Hortons everywhere.

The iconic status of *Bluenose* is even celebrated in a fascinating Nova Scotia Archives online exhibit. The origin of the name, the Atlantic schooner tradition, the launch of *Bluenose I*, the famous trophy races, its elevation to showboat then its decline, decay and loss, are all recon-structed in epic fashion. Metaphor and identity are intertwined in weaving and contextualizing that popular narrative.

Today, *Bluenose* is revered by Nova Scotians and has achieved the status of a sacred trust, unsul-lied by the recent, seemingly never-ending, cost-overrun controversy. How *Bluenose* became a provincial deity is a story worth exploring and retelling. The celebrated racing ship and fishing vessel, built in Lunenburg in 1921 and sailing under the command of Angus Walters, achieved notoriety in the 1920s and became a recognizable Canadian symbol in the 1930s.

(Top) Atlantic Schooners. Official logo of proposed Halifax Canadian Football League team back in 1982-83.

(Left) The Captain and his Prize: Bluenose Skipper Angus Walters poses with the *Halifax Herald* International Fishermen's Race Trophy, circa 1921.

THE QUEEN

Dubbed by admirers as the "Queen of the North Atlantic," she served as a working vessel, achieved fame as the fastest fishing schooner and was wrecked at sea in 1946. She lived on as a symbol on the Canadian 10-cent coin and was commemorated by a replica, *Bluenose II*, built in 1963, and then reconstructed, through an arduous process, 40 years later.

The name "Bluenose" is distinctively Nova Scotian in origin. Noted Halifax historian Brian Cuthbertson dug deeply into the origin of the term and discovered that it has been a nickname applied to Nova Scotians since the late 18th century.

The nickname Bluenose or Bluenoser may have been coined by a long forgotten British Empire Loyalist clergyman, Reverend Jacob Bailey, in letters written back in 1785 drawing a distinction between newly arrived Loyalists (or Tories) and the longer-established New England planters, labelled 'blue noses.'

It popped up again in Thomas Chandler Haliburton's 1838 classic, *The Clockmaker*, as a label applied by the fictionalized Yankee travelling salesman Sam Slick and used to describe native Nova Scotians. While originally invoked as "an appellation of derision," it gradually lost that connotation and became more of a colloquial expression of endearment.

The famous Lunenburg schooner was certainly not the first Nova Scotian entity to be called Bluenose. The name caught on so much from the 1850s onward that Bluenose was the name affixed to many more publications, companies, businesses, railways and boats. A Halifax-based magazine in 1853 was named the *Blue-nose*, and so was a Digby newspaper in the 1860s and 1870s. *The Flying Bluenose* was an express train operated in 1891 by the Windsor and Annapolis Railway, and a New Glasgow mining enterprise in 1896 bore the name Bluenose Gold Mining Company.

FASTEST VESSEL IN THE FLEET

While the name Bluenose became commonplace, bestowing it upon the famous Grand Banks fishing schooner ensured it would be the most famous Nova Scotian icon of them all.

Leading Nova Scotia citizens played a pivotal role in establishing the fishing boat races that *Bluenose* eventually came to dominate. Under the leadership of Senator William H. Dennis, owner of Halifax Herald Limited and publisher of the *Halifax Herald* and *Halifax Mail* newspapers, a group of civic-minded businessmen and sportsmen established the International Fishermen's Race and a *Halifax Herald* trophy was donated to be awarded annually to the fastest vessel in the North Atlantic fishing fleet.

The original *Bluenose* schooner was launched with great expectations on March 26, 1921 in Lunenburg. It was designed by William Roué and built by local shipbuilders at the Smith and Rhuland Shipyard. *Bluenose* Captain Angus Walters and the builders who crafted the visually appealing vessel were visionaries, setting their sights on building the fastest schooner in the North Atlantic.

The International Fishermen's Race became the supreme test for such a sailing vessel. For a working fishing schooner like the *Bluenose*, speed was all important because the boat that made it back to port first fetched the best price for their catch.

Bluenose was conceived as a speedy fishing vessel rather than a showpiece among the elite class of sailing yachts. It competed in The Fishermen's Race, a rough and ready competition for the hard-working vessels of fishermen who made their living on the sea. With every race, it seemed as though Nova Scotia's pride and shipbuilding reputation rode on the performance of *Bluenose*.

Bluenose's race victories in the 1920s and 1930s were the stuff of sailing legend. In October of 1921, the Nova Scotian *Bluenose* defeated the Gloucester schooner *Elsie* and took home her first Fisherman's Trophy. During the next 17 years, no challenger — American or Canadian — could wrest the trophy from *Bluenose*. In 1926, a dispute erupted between the Lunenburg and Gloucester fishing-fleet communities, leading to separate races and diminishing the honour of winning the annual racing event. Without the international competition, *Bluenose* retained the title "Queen of the North Atlantic" and became a powerful little symbol of Nova Scotia's fishing and racing prowess.

(Left) Launch of *Bluenose II*, 1963: Captain Angus Walters dives home the first golden spike on February 27, 1963 at the keel laying of the replica *Bluenose II*. Designer of the original *Bluenose*, Bill Roue, stands behind the Captain, while (left to right) Victor Oland, Fred Rhuland, and Col. Sidney Oland look on at the Lunenburg Harbour pier.

TOUGH COMPETITION

Bluenose faced stiffer challenges in 1930 and 1931. Competing in the Sir Thomas Lipton Cup out of Gloucester, Massachusetts, against a brand-new schooner the *Gertrude L. Thebaud*, the Lunenburgers suffered their first setback. That loss was avenged a year later in the revived International Fishermen's Race, but the Nova Scotia vessel was showing her age and her times were disappointing.

The Great Depression dealt a severe blow to the salt-fish trade. *Bluenose*, like many fishing vessels, fell on hard times. Capitalizing on the vessel's celebrity status, the Bluenose Schooner Company switched gears and sought to make money by touring the schooner as one of the last, and possibly greatest, of the remaining 'salt-bankers.'

The commodification of *Bluenose* soon followed. Promotional products, including a souvenir booklet and a puzzle, were produced to raise funds for a showboat tour and commercial sponsors climbed on board, sensing the marketing opportunities. The *Halifax Herald*, once again, rallied to the cause and actively promoted *Bluenose* in its pages as a travelling ambassador of Nova Scotia.

WELL! HERE'S HOPING, YOUR EXCELLENCY!

(Right) Well, Here's Hoping, Your Excellency! *Halifax Herald* political cartoonist Donald McRitchie depicts Governor-General, The Duke of Devonshire, driving the first spike for the original *Bluenose*, promoted by the *Halifax Herald* as Canada's hope in the inaugural international fishing schooner race.

(Halifax Herald, December 20, 1920)

Saves Bluenose

ap'n Angus Pays $7000
Ine Hour Before Auction

LUNENBURG, Nov. 14.— Captain Angus Walters came to the rescue of the Bluenose today when he placed $7000 on the Sheriff's desk one hour before the Queen of the North Atlantic fishing fleet was to be auctioned. Sale of the schooner had been ordered by the courts in an action for debt, at the suit of the Canadian Fairbanks Morse Co., Ltd., whose claim was for the amount of $7000 the balance due on the cost of engines installed in the schooner three years ago.

Capt. Walters said: "I would not see the schooner ld which so faithfully served me, the town of Lunenburg nd the owners for over 18 years." The Bluenose is still owned the Bluenose Schooner mpany of which Zwicker d Company are the chief areholders.

THE BLUENOSE

"I have faith in the Blue-se and will have for some me to come and I think it a sgrace the schooner should ave been threatened with e auction block. I still will otect the Bluenose with all have as she served me too ithfully to be let down," apt. Walters declared.

He said the Bluenose may fishing in the Spring and lded the plan originated by committee of public spirited men in Lunenburg to take over e Bluenose and preserve her as a memorial had fallen rough.

CAPT. ANGUS WALTERS

(Herald Archives)

(Top) Saving *Bluenose*, 1939: A *Halifax Herald* news story on November 15, 1939 reports on Captain Angus Walters' last minute intervention to save *Bluenose* from going to auction.

Bluenose came to symbolize Nova Scotia's traditions and prominence in the fishing and shipbuilding industries. She represented Nova Scotia and Canada around the world. In 1933, *Bluenose* appeared at the Century of Progress World's Fair in Chicago, and sailed to the Silver Jubilee of King George V and Queen Mary in England in 1935. The elderly king was too frail to board the vessel, but still paid tribute to *Bluenose* as "a vessel of considerable merit typical of the spirit of Nova Scotians."

Bluenose achieved its greatest recognition as it approached its racing retirement. In January 1929, the Canadian Postal Service issued a *Bluenose* 50-cent stamp depicting the Nova Scotia vessel under full sail passing the famous American schooner *Columbia* at sea. It returned in 1982 on a 37-cent stamp and was featured along with skipper Angus Walters on a 1988 commemorative issue.

The fishing schooner on the Canadian dime, issued in 1937 at the height of *Bluenose's* fame, was actually based upon a composite image of *Bluenose* and two other schooners. The artist, Emmanuel Hahn, confirmed this fact, but in 2002 the Canadian government bowed to public sentiment and declared the image to be that of *Bluenose*.

THE WAR YEARS

The Second World War wreaked havoc with the North Atlantic sea lanes and the collapse of the Grand Banks fishery spelled trouble for *Bluenose* and other similar vessels. In 1939, the Queen of the North Atlantic Fleet was tied up at the wharf in Lunenburg and faced the auction block. It was saved temporarily by Captain Walters for a claiming price of $7,000.00.

In 1942, the original *Bluenose* was finally sold to the West Indian Trading Company and became a rather gritty roving tramp schooner carrying goods throughout the Caribbean. It struck a coral reef off Ile a Vache, Haiti, in January 1946, and was wrecked beyond repair, sinking to the bottom of the sea.

Bluenose rose again in 1963 in the form of a replica, *Bluenose II*, built by Smith and Rhuland using the original plans and financed by the Oland Brewing Company. Conceived of as a marketing tool for the Oland Brewery Schooner Lager beer brand, it also served as the personal yacht for the Oland family of Halifax and Saint John, NB. In 1971, the Government of Nova Scotia purchased *Bluenose II* for the sum of $1 or the equivalent of 10 Canadian dimes. The replica schooner was used as a tourist attraction and adopted as the province's so-called "sailing ambassador."

Bluenose mystique is not always enough to carry a project through to completion. A stylized version of *Bluenose* was adopted as the symbol of the Atlantic Schooners, a proposed Canadian Football League (CFL) expansion team, in November 1982. The Halifax-Dartmouth team ownership failed to secure funding for a stadium and the franchise application was withdrawn in June 1983, 13 months after it had been submitted to the CFL.

Like its namesake, *Bluenose II* presented problems when it reached its life expectancy. It proved costly to maintain and underwent several refits to extend its life. In 2010, the replica was decommissioned and dismantled for what Transport Canada deemed a "reconstruction." In 2013, the Nova Scotia government stepped in to take charge of the project.

Four years of a major refit resulted in cost overruns, delays and much public controversy. Costs soared over those four years from $14 million to some $25 million, and by July of 2014 the rebuilt vessel with a steel rudder was still not cleared to leave the dock. The "never-ending refit has," Rob Gordon wrote in *The Globe and Mail*, "turned Nova Scotia's fabled icon into a national embarrassment."

A succession of Nova Scotia cabinet ministers and senior civil servants rode out the storm of criticism. After several shaky test runs and further repairs to the steering operation, the restored *Bluenose II* embarked on a tour of Nova Scotia ports in the summer of 2015.

The Stephen McNeil government launched an $870,000 Canada 150 public relations initiative in early 2017 to restore the shine on *Bluenose's* tarnished image. The centrepiece of that government-sponsored campaign was a geodesic-dome exhibit with a sound and light show featuring a 45-minute documentary film, *Project Bluenose: The Legend Lives*, and paying homage to the popular mythology.

The new *Bluenose II* was seaworthy in time for the Tall Ships Sail Past in Halifax Harbour on August 1, 2017. When it came into view, leading the parade of ships, a loud cheer erupted on dockside, emanating loudest of all from a party of Nova Scotia politicians and dignitaries atop the Seaport Farmers' Market. Nothing, it seems, can dampen the enthusiasm of Nova Scotians for this little fishing schooner.

Digging Deeper – for Further Reading

Cuthbertson, Brian, Johnny Bluenose at the Polls. Halifax: Formac Publishing, 1994.

De Villiers, Marq, Witch in the Wind: The True Story of the Legendary Bluenose. Toronto: Thomas Allen, 2007.

McLaren, R. Keith, A Race for Real Sailors: The Bluenose and the International Fishermen's Race 1920-1938. Vancouver: Douglas & McIntyre, 2005.

Nova Scotia Archives and Records Management, Bluenose: A Canadian Icon. Halifax: Nova Scotia Archives. novascotia.ca/archives/bluenose (Accessed 9/28/2017)

Robinson, Ernest Fraser, The Saga of the Bluenose. St. Catharines, ON: Vanwell Publishing, 1998.

Turning Point 6

North Atlantic Line of Defence:
Halifax at War, 1939-1945

(Opposite) Convoy of Merchant Ships and Naval Escorts in the Bedford Basin, circa 1941. The Bedford Basin was a prime staging area for the convoys preparing to embark across the dangerous waters of the North Atlantic to Britain.

On Sunday September 3, 1939, Nova Scotians opened the *Halifax Herald* main edition and could not miss the giant headline: "EMPIRE AT WAR." It was accompanied by a dramatic cut line that read "LINER ATHENA IS TORPEDOED AND SUNK."

After a daily drumbeat of headlines leading up to that day, most people sensed that a wider war was in the offing. A mere 20 years after the Great War, it produced more of a chill than a shock. On that day, Haligonians knew that Canada was at war, even though Canadian Prime Minister Mackenzie King maintained, for a full week, that the country was not until Parliament had spoken. Everywhere you looked, as historian William Naftel pointed out in his 2008 book *Halifax at War*, preparations for war were already underway.

Since the 1938 Munich Crisis and the contentious agreement to petition Czechoslovakia, the Royal Canadian Navy (RCN) had been clearing the decks for action. Local theatres were featuring the film, *Confessions of a Nazi Spy*, starring Edward G. Robinson. Two months before the outbreak, hundreds of Haligonians had shown up at the Bayer's Road municipal airport to watch a spirited drill of the newly formed First Anti-Aircraft Battery, the first such unit in Canada.

Unlike during the First World War, there was no public fanfare and no marching bands, but rather a silent gathering of a crowd along the waterfront to watch the modest RCN fleet put out to sea. Within a few short weeks, the streets of Halifax, once quiet and orderly, were crowded with thousands of servicemen, many of whom had, in Naftel's words, "little money and nothing to do."

A HEAVY PRICE

Patriotic euphoria gradually returned, but Halifax proved ill-prepared for the wartime surge of newcomers putting severe strains on housing, retail stores, healthcare and social services. It would not only produce what was described as "a severe case of indigestion," but also sow the seeds for rioting in the streets at war's end. The city paid a heavy price for its wartime role as the swollen crossroads of Canada.

When the war broke out in September 1939, the German navy, which had prepositioned U-boats (submarines) and powerful surface warships in the Atlantic, began to attack British merchant ships. As the Atlantic base of Canada's tiny navy, Halifax immediately became an indispensable Allied port from which to fight the Battle of the Atlantic.

The port city, in the eyes of the British, was the "Warden of the North." That description harkened back to Rudyard Kipling's poetic verse of the 1890s:

> Into the mist my guardian prows put forth,
> Behind the mist my virgin ramparts lie;
> The Warden of the honour of the North,
> Sleepless and veiled am I.

Halifax's reputation as Britain's most valuable wartime port was reaffirmed in 1939, and the British sent a strong force to Halifax for the protection of Atlantic shipping. Britain-bound merchant ships of many nationalities came to Halifax, where Bedford Basin provided a magnificent, secure anchorage in which ships could be organized into convoys, which then set out under the protection of Allied warships. The convoy system had also proven its worth during the First World War. HX-1, the first of the hundreds of convoys that would cross the Atlantic during the Second World War, sailed from Halifax on September 16, 1939.

THE THIRD LARGEST

From only 13 ships at the outbreak of war, the Royal Canadian Navy mushroomed to 332 warships, becoming the third largest Allied navy in the war. Coastal patrol ships known as corvettes were chosen by the RCN because they were simple-to-produce vessels and could be built cheaply by Canadian shipyards with no experience in naval construction.

Starting in May 1941, Canadian military authorities took the lead in building a new naval base at St John's, Newfoundland, and in supplying most of the warships that escorted convoys across the 3,000 kilometres of ocean between Newfoundland and the British Isles. When German U-Boats began to attack trans-Atlantic ships in "wolf packs," the corvettes were pressed into service as escort ships performing a vital role in keeping open the sea lanes by protecting convoys of merchant vessels transporting essential war supplies and foodstuffs to the United Kingdom.

The Halifax naval base retained its critical role with the additional responsibility of equipping and crewing the scores of new corvettes and minesweepers that arrived from builders along the St. Lawrence and on the Great Lakes. The old, cramped Royal Navy dockyard expanded with

(Right) Halifax Waterfront, January 1942. Wartime censor H.B. Jefferson captured the arrival of the SS *Queen of Bermuda* and ZOO HMCS *Acadia*.

(NSARM/ Nova Scotia Archives, H.B. Jefferson Photo Collection)

temporary buildings, and the navy took over adjacent army and municipal properties, which quickly became overcrowded as well.

The city's population mushroomed. In Halifax, it rose from 67,872 in 1939 to a peak of 106,742 in 1944. Across the harbour, Dartmouth almost doubled in population from 9,964 to 17,277. "Apartment for Rent" signs quickly disappeared from street-facing windows. The federal government focused most of its energies on mobilizing men and materials and was slow to respond to the serious problems of overcrowding and its attendant social ills. Local politicians were no better, refusing to respond with public housing until long after the war.

Herald reporter Eric Dennis, nephew of the legendary newspaper owner Senator William H. Dennis, had a close up, dockside view of the war. Rebuffed in his attempts to enlist, Dennis settled in to provide remarkably gritty, eye-witness reports for the morning *Herald* and its sister paper, the afternoon *Mail*.

Dennis was a working beat reporter who kept his nose to the ground and provided Nova Scotians with a steady diet of local exposes and wartime news. He figures prominently in Halifax journalism professor Stephen Kimber's highly acclaimed book, *Sailors, Slackers and Blind Pigs: Halifax at War*, and rightly so.

Drawing upon his five years of reporting experience, Dennis made good use of his network of contacts, ranging from the military brass and booze-can operators to baggage handlers, railway conductors and porters. He chaffed at wartime censorship, but — for the most part — played by the rules.

STRICT CENSORSHIP

On September 1, 1939, Mackenzie King's federal government passed Order-in-Council PC 2481, imposing strict censorship rules, and the Chief Censor for Canada, Wilfrid Eggleston, appointed Jeff Jefferson to oversee operations for the Maritimes, working out of Halifax. Press censorship in the region covered 16 daily newspapers, 10 radio stations, 77 weeklies, two wire services, a variety of magazines and newsletters as well as the reporting of visiting journalists filing stories elsewhere. Wielding a press prohibition stamp, he reviewed every news story or broadcast, in advance, and decided whether the story would — or should — be told.

The port city of Halifax lived under an assumed name during the Second World War. Under the censorship rules, newspapers like the *Herald*, *Mail* and *Chronicle* could no longer identify Halifax in their reportage and were required to report from "An East Coast Port." It was a rather phony ruse, however, because everyone, including the Germans, knew that it was actually Halifax and few were fooled by sanitized reports that completely disguised the existence of bars or taverns in the unnamed city.

The promised wartime industries, such as aircraft manufacture, which brought the best jobs and contracts, went largely to central Canadian cities. "The East Coast Port" boom largely benefitted hotels, restaurants, cafes, hostels, laundries, cinemas, dancehalls, groceries and dry goods stores. One exception was the Clark Ruse aircraft plant, employing hundreds of workers, including women.

At Clark Ruse, a sizable number of women worked not only in personnel services and the steno pool, but in non-traditional factory roles. Seventeen-year-old Clara MacCormack was trained by a Montreal woman to rivet pieces and panels on planes. "It was exciting," she recalled, "You used electric guns and drills and got used to it." My own mother, Grace (MacPhee) Bennett, vividly recalled the whistles and cat calls on the long walk to the factory's business office. The closing of the plant in 1944 put an end to such adventures, but signalled the approaching end of the war.

BURSTING AT THE SEAMS

Halifax at war was bursting at the seams and a bit of a shambles with many old, dilapidated wooden buildings. Crowding was everywhere. Every train that came into the station was full and it was nearly impossible to find a cab, since most of the pre-war cabbies had gone off to war, leaving the task to drivers who frequently gouged unsuspecting riders. Rooming houses were jammed with wartime guests and more than a few unscrupulous landlords put service-men's wives and families up in hallways, attics and dank cellars.

The acute housing shortage eventually prompted the Dominion government to act, primarily to provide accommodation for munitions workers. In 1941, the Wartime Housing Limited was incorporated, ostensibly to supply temporary accommodation for such workers. Within weeks, tenders were issued for the construction of 400 houses on the Halifax peninsula, and more were planned for Tuft's Cove and for workers at the Clark Ruse at Eastern Passage.

(Public Archives of Nova Scotia/PANS, David Hall Photo)

(Top) Burning Tram Car: The first sign of what would become the infamous Halifax Riot of May 7-8, 1945.

Trouble was brewing below the surface in the city. War enthusiasm and patriotism among civilians disintegrated as the war wore on into the 1940s. Overcrowding, booming trade in illegal liquor exemplified by "blind pigs," or illegal bars and sailors sleeping in doorways, were constant reminders of the military presence in the city.

Local citizens grew tired of long lineups at restaurants and stores, and overburdened services, and attributed it all to the military influx. Nighttime revelry and overflowing dancehalls disturbed what was once a rather genteel downtown. Stories circulated among Haligonians of everyday examples of snobby "Upper Canadian" attitudes, especially sneering references to the city's "toonerville trolleys."

None of this building tension was detected by either city or military leadership, which proved, in Naftel's words, "out of touch with the pressure cooker that was Halifax in 1945." It all burst into the open with the official announcement on May 7, 1945 of Victory in Europe.

HALIFAX RIOTS

When news hit Halifax on VE Day, it sparked an eruption known far and wide as the Halifax riots. Who was to blame remains a matter of continuing controversy. Naval personnel had been openly expressing their displeasure with the high rents, scarcity of services and official restrictions on liquor consumption in wartime Halifax. Local citizens were equally frustrated by the wartime crowds and the deterioration of living conditions.

Officialdom ignored the signs of trouble brewing in the city. Naval Commander Rear Admiral Leonard Warren Murray seriously underestimated the built-up frustrations of seamen and the potential for upheaval. For his part, Mayor John E. Lloyd discussed the potential for disorder in 1944, but put no firm plans in place.

(Right) Victory in Europe Day Rioters in the Street. Crowds of rioters poured onto Hollis Street between Blowers and Bishop, May 8, 1945.

(Public Archives of Nova Scotia/PANS, David Hall Photo)

(Public Archives of Nova Scotia/PANS, H.B. Jefferson Photo Collection)

(Top) Halifax VE-Day celebrations degenerated into street riots. A shocking scene showing the riot in which service personnel and citizens roamed the streets, drinking, smashing windows, looting businesses and setting fires.

The riots began at 10:30 am on Monday, May 7, when naval passengers seized control of a downtown-bound tramcar and with the help of hundreds of boisterous sailors on Barrington Street set the trolley on fire. Ten city police and 30 unarmed military police were unable to control the surging crowds. While the initial rioters pushed the tramcar south on Barrington, sailors and civilians started ransacking and looting Halifax liquor stores on Sackville, Hollis and Buckingham streets.

The riots expanded to envelop most of downtown Halifax. Fortified by liquor from the store raids, the rioters spent the whole night and much of the following day creating mayhem, now joined by as many as 10,000 naval personnel and fired-up civilians in smashing windows and looting downtown businesses. The Olands Brewery was overrun and the crowds inflicted some $5,000.000 in damages before it finally subsided.

Rear Admiral Murray finally intervened late on Tuesday rounding up the Naval Shore Patrol and calling in the Army to deploy 1,000 soldiers from Debert, NS, to patrol the streets. It was too little too late to stop the civic carnage. Three rioters died in the mayhem and, in the large-scale vandalism, in Halifax and Dartmouth, 564 businesses suffered damage and 207 shops were looted. The riots were front page news right across Canada and far beyond.

A Royal Commission of Investigation, established on May 10, 1945 and headed by Supreme Court Justice Roy Lindsay Kellock laid most of the blame on the Naval Command, citing the critical lack of planning and the inadequacy of the Naval Shore Patrol responsible for policing naval personnel in the city. The debate goes on as to who was really to blame for the major disruption.

(Left) Crowds and Line-Ups: A typical crowd of service personnel and civilians lined up in 1941 to enter the Orpheus movie theatre, Barrington Street, Halifax.

(Public Archives of Nova Scotia/PANS, E.A. Bollinger Collection)

ANOTHER BIG BANG

The war ended for Haligonians with a real bang, albeit a minor replay of the 1917 Explosion. On July 18, 1945, the Halifax Magazine on the Dartmouth side of the Bedford Basin was the scene of fires and explosions lasting for a full day. North End residents were ordered to leave their homes, but thousands ignored the directive and lined the shoreline to watch what looked like a spectacular display of fireworks.

Halifax found itself cast during the Second World War in the uneasy role of Atlantic crossroads for Canadians on the major supply and shipping routes. Most Haligonians, long-time residents and newcomers, experienced the war in more up-close-and-personal ways than those in other Canadian cities.

Great sacrifices were made by Haligonians who opened their doors to hordes of newcomers and endured six years of acute overcrowding. Many service personnel who returned home after the war complained about local conditions and showed little appreciation of the hospitality of Nova Scotians. After all the sacrifices, the blackened reputation caused by the Halifax Riots was a bitter pill to swallow.

Digging Deeper – for Further Reading

Fingard, Judith, Janet Guildford and David Sutherland, *Halifax: The First 250 Years*. Halifax: Formac Publishing, 1999. "Chapter 7: Wrestling with Adversity," 1918-1945.

Kimber, Stephen, *Sailors, Slackers and Blind Pigs: Halifax at War*. Toronto: Anchor Canada, 2003.

Milner, Marc, *North Atlantic Run: The Royal Canadian Navy and the Battle for the Convoys*. Toronto: University of Toronto Press, 1985.

Naftel, William D., *Halifax at War: Searchlights, Squadrons and Submarines, 1939-1945*. Halifax: Formac Publishing, 2008

Sarty, Roger, *Canada and the Battle of the Atlantic*. Montreal: Art Global, 1998.

OLIVIA DE H
LEW AY
The DARK MI

Free Pardon

IRENE DAVIS
DESMOND

VIOLA DESMOND

ROSELAND
THEATRE
NEW GLASGOW, NOVA SCOTIA
768929
30¢ ADMIT ONE 30¢
768929

CANADA P

Breaking the Colour Bar:
Viola Desmond's Act of Resistance, 1946 to Now

(Opposite) Cover of the Commemorative Stamp book for Viola Desmond, depicting the Roseland Theatre, the ticket in dispute, and the stamp.

Today Viola Desmond is a household name across Nova Scotia and far beyond. It all started on Friday, November 8, 1946 with a simple act of defiance in the face of overt racial discrimination. That racial incident in New Glasgow, made her an unlikely activist and eventually proved to be a pivotal turning point in the Black struggle to break the colour bar in Nova Scotia and Canada.

The whole episode, recounted in Viola's New Glasgow court testimony and in Constance Backhouse's 2001 legal history of racism in Canada, lives on today in a splendidly entertaining 2016 *Heritage Minute* re-enactment.

On that memorable day, Viola, at the time a petite and smartly dressed 32-year-old North End Halifax beautician and businesswoman, found herself waylaid for the night when her 1940 Dodge four-door sedan broke down en route to Sydney on a business trip. She decided to put in the evening by taking in the movie *Dark Mirror*, starring Olivia De Havilland and Lew Ayres, at the town's main entertainment venue, the Roseland Theatre.

Entering the theatre, Viola Desmond said to the cashier: "I'll have a ticket for downstairs, please." That was her normal practice because she was mildly nearsighted and liked to sit closer to the screen. The white ticket seller, Peggy Melanson, looked at her and gave her a ticket and 70 cents change.

'YOU CAN'T SIT HERE'

When Viola proceeded into the theatre and sat downstairs, a white usher, Prima Davis, tapped her on the shoulder and said: "Miss, you can't sit here because your ticket is for the upstairs balcony."

When Desmond attempted to change the ticket for one for downstairs, Melanson replied, "I'm sorry but I'm not permitted to sell downstairs tickets to you people." Desmond then acted, in spontaneous fashion, to take a seat again in the partially-filled downstairs section.

Viola's courageous action eventually provoked the theatre manager Harry MacNeil to call in the police. When the white police officer arrived, MacNeil and the policeman each took one of Viola's arms and forcibly dragged her out of the theatre. Roughed up and bruised, Desmond was locked up and placed alone in a small cell (in a jail with local drunks) for 12 hours before being released.

The next morning, November 9, 1946, Viola Desmond was brought before New Glasgow magistrate Roderick Geddes MacKay, charged with a violation of the provincial amusement tax law. The theatre manager claimed that Viola had purchased a ticket for the balcony but had taken a seat downstairs. The difference in price for the two tickets was 10 cents, and another one cent for the amusement tax.

Without legal counsel, Viola pleaded her own case, pointing out that she offered to pay the difference in price but was refused by the cashier. The magistrate disposed of the case quickly, convicting Desmond for failing to pay the one-cent amusement tax and assessing the minimum fine of $20, with costs of six dollars payable to the "informant," Harry MacNeil. Physically and emotionally shaken by the turn of events, she paid the fine (to avoid serving one month in jail) and left for home immediately after the ordeal.

(The Canadian Encyclopedia)

(Top) Viola Irene Davis Desmond – A portrait of Viola as she looked in the late 1940s at the time of the New Glasgow racial incident.

THE COLOUR BAR

Desmond's decision to challenge racial segregation in the courts made her one of the first Black women in Canada to do so. For many Nova Scotians, she came to symbolize what Backhouse described as "the essence of middle-class Black femininity" long before the American civil rights movement of the late 1950s and 1960s. Her civility, refinement and deportment in the face of outright discrimination also helped to raise awareness of the colour bar among the majority white community of Nova Scotians.

Taking action to protest racial discrimination in the mid-1940s did not win universal acceptance, even among African Nova Scotians. Her own husband, Jack Desmond, owner of Jack's Barber Shop and popularly known as "The King of Gottingen Street," was typical of many men of the time. He was not always supportive of her business travels and, in addition, expressed concern that raising a fuss might adversely affect his own business.

THE CLARION

Published in the Interest of Colored Nova Scotians

VOL. 1., NO. 1.   NEW GLASGOW, N. S.   DECEMBE..

Locals

The Season's Greetings to
All Our Readers

Mr. and Mrs. James MacPhee have moved into their new home on South Albert Street.

Calbert Best, student at King's College, Halifax, will spend the Christmas recess with his parents, Mr. and Mrs. A. T. Best.

Congratulations are being extended to Rev. and Mrs. Thomas for their Christmas Calendar. It is a lovely job!

Miss Evelyn Williams, daughter of Mr. Norman Williams, stenographer with the Pay Roll Depurment at Ottawa, will be home on Dec. 20th to spend the Christmas holidays with her family.

Friends will be interested to know that Miss Thelma Parris, formerly of this town, has become an American citizen. She is making her home in Cambridge, where her mother, Mrs. Douglas Gordon, resides.

The Ladies' Auxiliary of Second Baptist Church held a successful sale and tea in the Church Hall on Dec. 10th. A lovely display of fancy work was noted

Mr. and Mrs. Lemuel Mills left Saturday, Dec. 14, for Boston, where they will spend Christmas with their daughters, Mrs. Thornton Harper and Mrs. Bennie Shepherd.

Johnnie Mills met a deer—DEER, that is, recently, while driving his mother to Halifax. The deer darted out on the highway near Elmsdale and hit the side of the car. Not seriously injured, the deer soon scampered off, none the worse of the impact.

Word has been received that Miss Irma Halfkenney will be a participant in the St. John Music Festival in May. A student at Mount Allison School of Music, Miss Halfkenney is a soprano of promise, and that she will make a creditable showing goes without saying.

The Senior B. Y. P. U. of Second Baptist Church chartered a bus and motored to Riverton where they held a service for the inmates of the Pictou County Home. Among those who took part were Rev. H. D. Thomas, Howard Lawrence, Miss Althea Lawrence and Mrs. Gordon Clark. About twenty-five persons made the trip

The Ladies' Auxiliary of the Second Baptist Church had a surprise party early in December for Rev. and Mrs. Thomas, at the Parsonage, Washington St. The gifts included china, linen, etc., and each gift was accompanied by an original verse. Typical of the verses was the one accompanying the crocheted doily gift of President Mrs. L. Mills:

"I may be small, but my mission is great,
I'm here to decorate your cake plate,
Your cakes I know are a treat to eat,
So use me when next your guests you
   treat."

MRS. VIOLA DESMOND

Takes Action

Mrs. Viola Desmond, 32-year-old Negro Halifax beautician, arrested and fined $20 and costs by Magistrate Rod G. MacKay, of this town, for sitting downstairs in the Roseland Theatre while holding an upstairs ticket.

Mrs. Desmond was fined for defrauding the Federal Government of one cent, the difference in the Amusement tax on an upstairs ticket of two cents and a downstairs ticket of three cents.

Counsel for Mrs. Desmond, F. W. Bisset of Halifax, has served a writ against Henry MacNeil, manager of the theatre, charging false arrest, false imprisonment, assault and malicious persecution.

E. M. Macdonald, K.C., of New Glasgow, is acting for Mr. MacNeil.

Mrs. Desmond, the former Viola Davis, daughter of Mr. and Mrs. James Davis, of Halifax, is well known throughout the Province. She is a graduate of the Halifax High School, and is also a graduate in Beauty Culture from a leading Beauty College in New York. She is a niece of John Davis, Civil Service employee (Post Office Division), Halifax.

Viola Desmond's Appeal

Just as we go to press we are in receipt of a letter from Mrs. Bernice Williams, Sec'y N. S. A. A. C. P., informing us that an appeal trial of the Viola Desmond case will be held in Halifax on Dec. 27th, also a Viola Desmond Court Fund has been established by the Association soliciting contributions. A public meeting will be held by the Association on Dec. 22nd in Halifax asking everyone to attend and give their donation.

The N. S. A. A. C. P. is the Ladder to Advancement. STEP ON IT! JOIN TODAY!

Did You Know?

(a) That Adult education in rural communities is being sponsored by the N. S. A. A. C. P.

(b) That the Educational Department of the Province of Nova Scotia is supporting the movement.

(c) That a class has already started in Hammonds Plains and is progressing favourably.

(d) That the C.G. I. T. group of Cornwallis Street Baptist Church, Halifax, raised the sum of $35.00 at their Christmas Sale. Mrs. Oliver is leader and all girls are under 16 years.

(e) That the money will be used for the work of the Summer Camp at Fall River.

(f) That Mr. Horborn, of Fall River, gave the use of an island near the Cornwallis Street Church camp site for the promotion of the Young People's work of that Church.

(g) That two Colored girls are enrolled as student nurses in two Halifax hospitals. They are Miss Gwendolyn Barton of Halifax and Miss Ruth Bailley of Toronto.

(h) That J. Calbert Best of King's College, Halifax, will write for the Afro-American, one of the largest weekly Negro newspapers in the U. S. A. Mr. Best has been asked to prepare a 700-word article on Canada. The weekly circulation of the Afro is 200,000.

The N. S. A. A. C. P.

The Nova Scotia Association for the Advancement of the Colored People was organized in 1945:

(a) To improve and further the interest of the Colored people of the Province.

(b) To provide an organization to encourage and promote a spirit of fraternity among its members.

(c) To co-operate with Governmental and private agencies for the promotion of the interest and the welfare of the Province or any community therein, wherein Colored People are resident, and particularly in reference to said Colored people.

(d) To improve the educational opportunities of Colored youth and to raise the standard of the Colored people of the Province or any community therein.

The following people comprise the charter members of the Association:

Arnold P. Smith, Richard Symonds, William Carter, Bernice A. Williams, Carl W. Oliver, Walter Johnson, Pearleen Oliver, William P. Oliver and Ernest Grosse.

Join the N. S. A. A. C. P.
Write BERNICE A. WILLIAMS, Sec'y
166 Maynard Street.
Halifax, N. S.

Viola was not content to turn the other cheek in the face of such an injustice. She sought out the advice and counsel of leaders in the North End Black community, starting with Reverend William Pearly Oliver and his wife Pearleen Oliver. Seeking to gather support, Pearleen brought the case to the attention of the Nova Scotia Association for the Advancement of Coloured People (NSAACP).

With Pearleen Oliver leading the charge, the NSAACP overcame some initial reticence, including fears of a racial backlash, and eventually supported the cause. The NSAACP supported Desmond's case, Oliver told the *Halifax Chronicle*, to prevent "a spread of color-bar tactics" across the province.

When Desmond did speak out, it was more to express her dismay that racist measures like segregation existed in Canada. She told the *Halifax Chronicle* that, living in Halifax, it had "never happened to her before." Choosing her words carefully, Desmond expanded upon this observation, saying that she had always found relations between whites and Blacks to be "very pleasant" and expressed surprise that "a thing like this could happen in Nova Scotia — or in any other part of Canada." The ensuing court case, which lasted until, April 15, 1947, sapped her energy and losing the decision exacted its toll.

SISTER OF COURAGE

(Clarion Publishing, New Glasgow)

(Top) New Glasgow activist-editor Carrie M. Best and her paper, *The Clarion*.

The confident, defiant tone of the actress in the new *Heritage Minute* projects an image of Desmond as a vocal civil rights advocate. Her own sister, Wanda Robson, knew Viola better than anyone and offered a different interpretation. "I do not think that Viola was a social activist," Robson recalled in her 2010 memoir *Sister of Courage*. "She didn't plan to be one. Because her passion was not to right wrongs. But she was a brave and determined businesswoman — a singular one at that."

Following the disruption of the court case, Viola Desmond tried to get her life back on track. She gently rebuffed efforts by the NSAACP to go on a speaking tour and campaign for justice for Black Nova Scotians. Instead of continuing the fight, Viola began to pursue new business interests and dabble in real estate. A few years later, she closed her business, Vi's Studio of Beauty Culture, studied business in Montreal and moved to New York City to become an agent for entertainers.

Viola was not the first or the most outspoken Nova Scotian Black woman to stand up against racial prejudice. Four years before her protest, Carrie M. Best, a New Glasgow Black civil rights activist, had already challenged to no avail the practice of racial segregation at the Roseland Theatre.

Best was fierce in her defense of Desmond and in campaigning to rid Nova Scotia of racial segregation and discrimination. From her editorial perch as founding editor of the *New Glasgow Clarion*, she expressed alarm over suggestions that those who protest discrimination were "looking for trouble."

"Racial and Religious hatred," she wrote, "is trouble of the gravest kind. It is a vicious, smouldering and insidious kind of trouble born of fear and ignorance."

THE 'JIM CROW LAWS'

The editor of *The Clarion* laid bare the hidden face of Nova Scotia racism and its outward manifestation, segregation, reinforced by Nova Scotian variations on the so-called Jim Crow laws that persisted after emancipation in the American South. She profiled Viola Desmond's treatment on her front page, denouncing it as a "disgraceful incident," and expressing her view that "New Glasgow stands for Jim-crowism, at its basest, over the entire globe."

Legally enforced racial segregation did not survive the 1960s, but public attitudes changed with glacial speed in Nova Scotia. Not until April 2010, some 64 years after the Roseland Theatre incident and 45 years after Viola's passing, did justice come for Viola Desmond and her family. The Nova Scotia NDP government of Darrell Dexter finally made it right. On April 15, 2010, she was issued an official apology and granted a free pardon.

A highly respected African Nova Scotian, Lieutenant Governor Mayann Francis conferred her blessing. "This closes an erroneous chapter in the history of this province," Francis said, "and I am proud to be a part of it."

Today, Viola Desmond is experiencing something of a Nova Scotia renaissance. She is now being honoured as a Nova Scotia civil rights pioneer and adorns the Canadian $10 bill. Three recent books, Wanda Robson's *Sister to Courage* (2010), Graham Reynolds's *Viola Desmond's Canada* (2016), and Reynolds and Robson's *Viola Desmond: Her Life and Times* (2018) celebrate her life and help to solidify her reputation in the public eye. She now has a Dartmouth ferry bearing her name plying the waters in Halifax Harbour.

(Right) Souvenir Calendar Cover, Desmond's Barber Shop and Hairdressing, 1953.

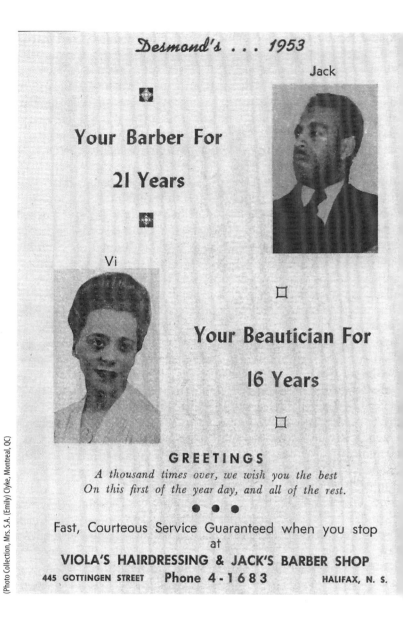

(Photo Collection, Mrs. S.A. (Emily) Clyke, Montreal, QC)

CARRYING THE TORCH

Viola's sister, Wanda Robson, has been carrying the torch in recent years. She was front-and-centre with Finance Minister Bill Morneau in early December 2016 when the government of Canada unveiled the new bill bearing her sister's face. "It's a really big day to have my big sister on a banknote," she said, describing Desmond as a "passionate" woman who cared deeply for people. "She inspired them as she inspires us."

(Photo Collection, Mrs. S.A. (Emily) Clyke, Montreal, QC)

Desmond is often compared with Rosa Parks, the American civil rights champion who in 1955, nine years after Desmond's action, refused to sit at the back of the bus in Montgomery, Alabama. Canada's largest daily newspaper, *The Toronto Star*, ran a late 2016 story calling Desmond "Canada's Rosa Parks." That diminishes, in some ways, Viola's courageous act, a decade earlier in Nova Scotia.

Who Viola Desmond was and what she means to Nova Scotians may be sinking in, even in the elementary grades. If that is so, then a recent Halifax Regional School Board project will have played a direct role in that consciousness raising.

On March 7, 2017, the school board, in co-operation with the Delmore Buddy Daye Learning Institute, launched a homegrown children's book, *ABCs of Viola Desmond*. Each letter of the alphabet was used to highlight an episode in the life of Desmond and students at William King Public School in Herring Cove provided their own short texts and illustrations. It's an instant bestseller now that copies have been distributed to every Grade 3 class in the school district. Scratch below the surface and a few uncomfortable realities come into sharper relief: the high numbers of African-Nova Scotian students on individual program plans (IPPs, for children identified as having "special education needs"), the disproportionate suspension rates and the high incidence of police street checks.

Renowned Canadian poet-novelist and proud African Nova Scotian George Elliott Clarke put it this way, in his introduction to *Viola Desmond's Canada:* "anti-racism in Canada succeeds when renegades' protests meet with, sooner or later, elite accommodation."

Viola Desmond's celebrated act of resistance was effective because it made a blatant discriminatory practice look ridiculous in the eyes of both Black and white Nova Scotians. In spite of the wide exposure, racism persisted albeit in a politer, less visible form. It was what Yale University political scientist James C. Scott once termed "an exceptional moment of popular explosion" that did not actually address the underlying ideology of racism or "tear at the fabric of hegemony."

Digging Deeper – for Further Reading

Backhouse, Constance, Colour-Coded: A Legal History of Racism in Canada, 1900 -1950. Toronto: Osgoode Society for Legal History, 2001.

Best, Carrie M., That Lonesome Road: An Autobiography. New Glasgow, NS: Clarion Publishing, 1977. Reynolds, Graham, Viola Desmond's Canada: A History of Blacks and Racial Segregation in the Promised Land. Halifax: Fernwood Publishing, 2016.

Robson, Wanda, Sister to Courage: Stories from the World of Viola Desmond, Canada's Rosa Parks. Sydney, NS: Breton Books, 2010.

Scott, James C., Domination of the Arts of Resistance. New Haven: Yale University, 1990.

Walker, James W. St. G., The Black Identity in Nova Scotia: Community and Institutions in Historical Perspective. Dartmouth, NS: Black Cultural Centre for Nova Scotia, 1985.

Grim Survivor

BILL MILLER, father of four children, is grim-faced after his rescue from the pit. He and several others were working at the 13,800-foot level when the bump clogged the shaft with rock. He was rescued by draegermen.

N.S. MINE 93 BURIED ALIVE

METRO EDITION

TORONTO DAILY STAR

Authorized as second-class mail, Post-Office Department, Ottawa.

FRIDAY, OCTOBER 24, 1958—68 PAGES   10c PER COPY   55c PER WEEK BY HOME DELIVERY

THE WEATHER
Toronto and vicinity — Scattered showers today and Saturday. Low tonight, 45; high Saturday, 55.

THE DRAEGERMEN, Nova Scotia's famed mine rescue crews, are working unceasingly in an attempt to reach miners trapped in No. 2 colliery of the Cumberland mine at Springhill. In 1956, two draegermen lost their lives during rescue operations in the mine's No. 4 shaft in which 39 miners died. William James is shown trying to comfort relatives crowding around pithead last night following rock fall. He and other draegermen rescued some within 15 minutes

93 Buried Under Mountains of Dust Two-Week Task

By ROBERT MACDONALD
Star Staff Correspondent

Springhill, N.S., Oct. 24—There is only "the vaguest glimmer of hope" of finding alive any of 93 coal miners trapped in the underground ruins of Cumberland No. 2 colliery.

This was the grim word today from Harold Gordon, general manager of coal operations of Dominion Steel and Coal Co. after eight gruelling hours underground directing rescuers.

Another top company official said it will be "at least one week and possibly two" before the missing men can be reached.

The missing men are among 173 miners who were in the three working levels of the colliery last night when a sudden "bump" spewed destruction through North America's deepest coal mine. Seventy-nine men reached the surface safely, of whom 16 were injured and rushed to hospital. The body of one man was recovered.

Mr. Gordon, with tears in his eyes and his voice breaking, said: "I regret very much but I consider there is no hope for any man."

He explained hope was dimmed because the men are not—as in mine disasters—trapped. He believed they were buried alive under mountains of coal dust.

Mr. Gordon described the search for the buried men as a slow, painful process. But, he said, rescue teams will continue their inch-by-inch advance into the disintegrated mine workings "until we get every man out."

ON THREE LEVELS

The missing men are on all three working levels—at 13,000, 13,400 and 13,800 feet. The levels extend from a long sloping shaft, which extends at a 30-degree angle from the surface.

Fifty-five of the missing are on the 13,000-foot level. But, because of the cramped quarters only a single draegerman crew of five men is able to work on the level at a time. Here, they face the additional hazard of a wall of poisonous gas. The oxygen masks they must wear under such conditions slow their progress.

No rescue work is underway at the 13,800-foot level. However, at the 13,400-foot level, where gas is not a hazard, rescuers are fighting through debris.

To help them, crews of draegermen are rushing to the scene from other collieries in Pictou county and Cape Breton island.

Company officials reported that, an aid to the search, is the fact that the ventilation system is still working on all three levels.

Mr. Gordon said the "bump" was the first one he had known of in 30 years of mining to occur at a working face of a mine. The effect of the "bump", a surge from the floor of the working face, was to hurl everything upwards, including the heaviest underground equipment. Timbers collapsed, the roof caved in and men were buried in a sea of coal dust.

KNOW LOCATION OF 55

Rescue workers have determined the location of 55 men on the 13,000-foot level. But they're still uncertain of where the other missing men are.

Mr. Gordon explained the "bump" occurred from the release of pressures built up between harder rock overhead and the softer underfloor strata.

Manson Harrison, one of the survivors, told company officials he
(Continued on Page 9, Column 1)

STAR APOLOGY TO DAVID J. WALKER

On August 25 and August 28 of this year, The Toronto Star published two editorials dealing with the proceedings of the Public Accounts committee of the House of Commons which was then investigating the costs of the new Printing Bureau building at Hull. These two editorials criticized severely the conduct of David J. Walker, Q.C., M.P., the counsel who was conducting the investigation on behalf of David J. Walker. Those two editorials criticized severely the conduct of David J. Walker, Q.C., M.P., the counsel who was conducting the investigation on behalf of the steering committee consisting of representatives of the three parties.

In effect, the editorials accused Mr. Walker of using unfair tactics in his examination of civil servants, of bullying and displaying rudeness to civil servants and using third-degree methods in his examination of twenty-six volumes of evidence of this investigation now indicates that these charges against Mr. Walker were unfounded.

The editorials also suggested that Mr. Walker would not allow his political career to be held back by a sense of fair play. This comment was improper and unjustified. Accordingly The Toronto Star gladly publishes this explanation and apology and expresses its regrets to Mr. Walker for the embarrassment which these articles caused him. The Star has reservations about the manner in which the committee conducted the inquiry and believes that the committee should have followed the well established principles of the British Public Accounts committee.

Always 2 Years Behind Monty Blaming U.S. For World Troubles

London, Oct. 24—(Reuters)—Field Marshal Viscount Montgomery said today that the United States must shoulder "a large proportion, perhaps most, of the blame" for the present world situation.

The 71-year-old military hero ripped into U.S. foreign policy—and that of Britain under its former Labor government—in a lecture at the Royal United Services institution here.

In a reference to the Anglo-French Suez intervention of 1956, Montgomery declared: "If the United States had not sabotaged the Suez operation and had joined the Bagdad Pact earlier, the situation in the Middle East would have been very different."

The U.S. is not a full member of the pact, although it belongs to all its main committees.

Montgomery, who retired a month ago from the British army and as a deputy supreme Allied commander in Europe, asserted American foreign policy was inconsistent.

"Washington seemed to have one policy in the United Nations and another when its own national interests were involved.

The U.S. supported ex-colonial powers in western

Europe but worked to destroy their influence in Africa.

As a result there had been a decline in much of the Dutch, French and British empires which should have been stabilizing influences in the post-war period.

Montgomery asserted that during the war Britain and the U.S. failed to take the necessary political steps to win the peace after it became apparent Nazi Germany would be defeated.

Britain had to take "first blame" for this. The world but the post-war labor government concentrated on creating a welfare state and economic condition, reflecting world affairs.

The "second degree" of blame must be placed on the U.S. to which world leadership had passed after Britain "declined" it.

The U.S., the field marshal said, always ran two years behind in its understanding of Europe.

It was two years before the United States joined the two World Wars, two years before it realized the full implication of the Soviet vision and more than two years before it fully supported the Bagdad Pact.

All In Rome Busy Trying To Outguess Cardinals On Pope

By DAVID MacDONALD
Star Staff Correspondent

Rome, Oct. 24—At Vatican workmen add final Italian flourishes to Michelangelo's Sistine chapel — that elaborate polling place where 52 cardinals of the Roman Catholic church will tomorrow or a day or a new Pope—almost everyone else in Rome is busy second-guessing the august electors.

In the press, on street corners, around the city's 400 churches and in equally numerous sidewalk cafes, Papal speculation has been mounting steadily since the death of Pope Pius XII two weeks ago.

At times it has seemed like the prelude to a rousing political convention, rather than a solemn gathering of the world's most venerable secular — the reason why the Vatican newspaper "l'Osservatore Romano" recently commanded the faithful: "Abandon prognostications on the conclave."

The conclave is due to begin
(Continued on Page 2, Col. 1)

THE WEATHER

FRIDAY-SATURDAY

Friday and vicinity forecast is: Cloudy with scattered showers and a few sunny intervals today, Saturday cloudy with a few scattered showers and sunny intervals; cooler Saturday. Winds light today, northwest 15 Saturday.

Mean yesterday, 56; 8 above average.
High yesterday, 2 p.m., 59.
Low yesterday, 8.10 a.m., 53.
Low today to 8 a.m., at 6.30.

Low since 1841 (1841), 21.
High since 1841 (1899), 70.
Wind: Yesterday, 8 a.m., NE 2; 2 p.m., E; 8 p.m., SE 2.
Rainfall for last 24 hours, .07.

[weather data table]

SUSPEND BELL RATE INCREASE FOR ONE MONTH

From The Star's Ottawa Bureau
Ottawa, Oct. 24—The federal government today suspended for one month the $17,150,000 Bell Telephone rate increase scheduled to go into effect Nov. 1.

The increase was approved only two weeks ago by the board of transport commissioners and an appeal taken against it to the cabinet by a number of provinces and municipalities in Ontario and Quebec.

The prime minister said the government "had decided... to suspend the increase to make it possible for the government to make an appraisal that have been made against it."

MINE PICTURES STORIES ON PAGES

2, 3, 8, 9, 10, 11

Other pictures and stories of last night's mine disaster for one month in the Springhill mine at Springhill, N.S., may be found on pages 2, 3, 8, 9, 10 and 11.

FOG GROUNDS PLANE

Star's MacDonald First At Springhill

The only Toronto newspaperman on the scene of tragedy at Springhill mine disaster last night and up until noon today was Robert MacDonald of The Star, a native of the Maritimes and one who knows the others and the men who work in these eight-man team of reporters and photographers which now arrived on the scene.

Dramatic first-hand accounts and vivid pictures of rescue operations are being wired and wirephoted to The Star by an eight-man team of reporters and photographers which now arrived on the scene.

Fog cancelled all flights last night and planes were grounded at Toronto, London and Montreal.

AMOK KILLS 4

Rome, Oct. 24—(AP)—Italian - immigrant Alfredo Seda ran amok with a shotgun Wednesday night, killing four persons in a family vendetta.

Amusements—43-44
Births, Deaths—47
Bridge—34
Comics—44-45
Crossword—45

INDEX

Horoscope—39
Markets—38-41
Racing—34
Radio, TV—36

Shipping—38-39
Sports—30-31
Suburban—42-46
Want Ads—47-54
Women—32-35

Turning Point 8

Springhill Mining Disaster:
A Bump Heard Around the World, 1958

On Thursday, October 23, 1958, coal mine Number 2 in Springhill, Nova Scotia experienced a tremendous bump. At around 8:05 pm families in the wooden houses throughout town were huddled around their new television sets watching *I Love Lucy* and laughing at the antics of the show's star, Lucille Ball. Then, all of a sudden, it hit, without warning, and for a 15-mile (23-km) radius the ground shook and the mine caved in, trapping 174 miners far below the surface.

The only working mine left in Springhill, Number 2, was reputed to be the deepest coal mine in operation in North America. From the pit head to the bottom of the mine was a distance of 2.7 miles (4.3 km), straight down. Having first opened in 1873, the mine was old, and that meant that mining operations were carried on at great depth below ground. Pressure had built up on the mineshafts in Number 2 and as coal was removed, gas was being released underground, and bumps or violent lurches were becoming increasingly common. Some 525 bumps had occurred before this one.

'THE GROUND SHOOK'

The power of the disturbance was incredible, and graphically illustrated in the Royal Commission report that followed the Springhill Mining Disaster. Mining underground, the bump hit with the force of "one thousand tons of coal being dropped 40 feet onto the ground." The ground shook with tremors detected at Dalhousie University's Seismograph Station, 119 kilometres away, and picked up on instruments as far away as Quebec City and Ottawa.

(Left) A group of coal miners pictured in the aftermath of the Springhill Bump in 1958.

One of the veteran miners and a survivor, Maurice Ruddick of Joggins, NS, had a premonition. "I told a fellow not long before it happened that a bad one was coming." Then why did he continue to go down to the deeps? It was, he said, for the "comradeship," but the truth was that there was little work to be found outside of the mines.

Coal was once king in the local economies of Nova Scotia outside of Halifax. Exploring the mining experience was, in a phrase popularized in John DeMont's memorable 2009 book, like a journey into "the coal black heart" of the province.

Without coal, DeMont reminds us, Nova Scotia outside the city "might still be just a collection of scattered farms and fishing villages." Mining gave Nova Scotians, he added with a lyrical flair, "a sense of urgency" and a "spirit forged by a flame that comes from betting everything, year after year, on the vagaries of a single commodity."

Townsfolk in Springhill lived on the edge in the 1950s. Shipping coal out on the rail line to markets in Ontario and Quebec had transformed Springhill into a mining boomtown by the 1890s. A sleepy hamlet of 900 souls had swelled to five times that size.

The first of its mining disasters hit in on Saturday February 21, 1891, when an underground explosion claimed the lives of 125 men and boys who worked in the mines. Money and aid came pouring in, totaling $70,000, mostly from larger Canadian centres and cities as far away as London, England.

The resilient town recovered from what Halifax newspapers described in late February 1891 as "the Springhill Calamity." A year later, an electric light system was installed. The loss of 182 more lives in some 125 separate accidents between 1892 and 1956 left Springhill bruised but not beaten. Townsfolk weathered a 1909 to 1911 coal mine strike and heavy losses in the two world wars. By the time of a 1956 explosion disaster the population stood at 8,000 with 1,585 employed in two mines, 1,200 of whom worked underground.

Somehow 19-year-old miner Ken Melanson survived the 1956 mine explosion. His harrowing story, nicely reconstructed by John DeMont, conveys deep insights into the subterranean life of a coal miner. The son and grandson of miners, Ken fell into that life as the better of two life options, earning $9.74 a day in the mines or settling for $4 a day in the woods. He tried his luck going down the road to Toronto, but — after four months of washing dishes — returned home.

(Below) The Last Man Out: A rather blurry photo of the last man rescued after the Springhill Disaster, November 1, 1958.

(Nova Scotia Archives)

TRAPPED

His life almost came to an end on a beautiful autumn day, Thursday November 1, 1956, when he was one of 47 miners trapped after the underground explosion. His shift supervisor-tuned-saviour, Com Embree, built a protective barrier and diverted away the poisonous gas. After being trapped for more than 60 hours, Ken Melanson and his group were rescued by the Springhill draegermen and emerged with blacked face to learn that 39 of his comrades had died in that explosion.

The Big One known as the "Springhill Mining Disaster" came two years later. At 8:06 on October 23, 1958, the moment of the disastrous bump, some 174 miners were toiling underground. Seventy-five of them trapped in Mine No. 2 lost their lives, and 88 would eventually be rescued from that underground tomb.

After the shaking in the town had stopped, a mad rush to the mine began, recounted in detail by Roger David Brown in his aptly titled 1976 book, *Blood on the Coal*. The resident mine manager, George Calder, arrived first on the scene and began mobilizing rescue operations. The volunteer rescue crew, led by Calder, ventured down to the bottom and discovered it blocked by debris and were driven back by methane gas.

(Right) Faces of Springhill Survivors: Two rescued miners, Bill Miller and Don Ferguson, rest in the change house after coming up from Mine No. 2 on October 24, 1958. The terror of the ordeal is shown on their soot stained faces.

(FEDNEWS Te ephoto)

'A PILE OF SPAGHETTI'

One miner put it succinctly: "The situation's terrible." A Springhill rescue worker was more graphic in describing the rubble: "It looks like a pile of spaghetti down there."

On Friday morning, October 24, the *Halifax Chronicle Herald* reported the dramatic news that some 72 men had been rescued alive and nine more were found to be dead upon discovery. "I don't think there is much hope for them," said one 14-year-old lad who did lose his father. The total number of miners rescued alive would reach 81 before the day was over.

(Library and Archives Canada)

(Left) Consoling a Rescued Miner after Springhill Mine Disaster, following the October 1958 mine collapse.

On the following Wednesday, six days after the mine collapse, buried miners were huddled underground, breathing through makeshift air pipes and tapping away in an attempt to send signals upward. Miner Gorley Kempt heard a pick or something click on the pipe and he started hollering.

The *Chronicle Herald* covered the rescue in minute detail and captured the moment when the last group was discovered. At about 2:00 am, the superintendent and an engineer checked the air coming from the pipe pushed through to the exposed surface. The reflection of a bottle sent a shaft of light into the pipe. It was Kempt who first broke the silence: "We are alive in here — how about some water?"

A PRINCELY VISIT

The disaster attracted worldwide media attention and even prompted a fly-in visit by His Royal Highness, Prince Philip. While en route from Ottawa back to London, he stopped in Moncton bound for Springhill. He was greeted by an official delegation, headed by Springhill Mayor R.F. Gilroy and including Nova Scotia Premier Robert Stanfield, federal Revenue Minister George Nowlan, and the Springhill MLA, Stephen Pyke, then Minister of Labour and Public Works.

The two-car convoy headed straight to the Springhill All Saints Hospital. After talking to the survivors one at a time, the Prince was briefed at the mine by Dosco Mining Company's general manager on the rescue operations. After his two-and-a-half hour whirlwind visit, the Prince whisked past Springhill children dressed in their Halloween costumes on the journey back to Moncton airport.

Underground, unbeknown to the Prince or the searchers, another group of buried miners had yet to be found. Far below, a small band of survivors, dubbed the Group of Seven, was still alive, a week after the bump.

Thirty-five-year-old Herb Pepperdine survived the bump after being thrown six or eight feet downhill by the force of the jolt. Slowly the group of seven gathered and huddled together, entertained by sing-songs and drinking oil and eventually urine to stay hydrated in the sweltering heat of the collapsed shaft. Worried about leaving behind his wife and 12 children, Maurice Ruddick passed the time singing some of his favourite songs.

THE GROUP OF SEVEN

Nine days after the disaster, given up for dead, the Group of Seven were rescued and raised to the surface. The first man out was Byron Martin, found alone, moaning in "a little hole." When Ruddick made contact with his rescuers, dazed by the nightmare, he blurted out "Give me a drink of water and I'll sing you a song."

The famous Springhill Group of Seven, instantly crowned the "miracle miners," were marked by that horrendous nine-day experience their whole lives. In a riveting 2003 book by American author Melissa Faye Green, *Last Man Out*, we learn more about what befell the unlikely band of instant heroes. Some were tormented by survivor's guilt, struggling with post-rescue depression; a few experienced an epiphany and attempted to change the course of their lives. Still others were swept up by forces beyond their control.

One of the most bizarre outcomes was a dramatic act of American generosity that went terribly wrong. The global spotlight on the rescue of the first group in newspapers, television news reports and movie theatre news reels catapulted miners onto CBS-TV's *Ed Sullivan Show*. In a strange twist, it also inspired a few highly placed officials in the administration of Georgia Governor Marvin Griffin, a staunch segregationist, to invite the survivors and their families to vacation on the coastal resort of Jekyll Island, Georgia. It was, it turned out, a publicity stunt, dreamed up by Georgia state officials, to market the Georgia coast as an alternative to Florida's beaches.

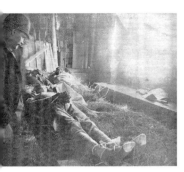

(The Dominion Illustrated, March 7, 1891, Nova Scotia Archives)

(Top) Victim of Springhill 1891 Explosion: A rare photo of a victim in the makeshift morgue following the infamous 1891 explosion that claimed 125 lives.

The discovery of the second group of survivors presented Governor Griffin with a dilemma. The "last man out" was Maurice Ruddick, an African-Nova Scotian. Since all tourist accommodations in Georgia were segregated, state officials scrambled to find 'alternative' arrangements for Ruddick in a trailer camp at the end of the beach.

The invited Springhill guests initially balked at the trip because of the state's policy, but Ruddick eventually wavered and this persuaded his fellow survivors to take up the offer. News coverage in Canada and elsewhere drew attention to the living example of racial injustice and it was blown up in the press as an international incident.

'THE SINGING MINER'

The media, desperate for a hero, seized upon Ruddick, labelling him with the moniker "The Singing Miner," and inflating his role in the drama. When the *Toronto Telegram* polled its readers for their choice as "Canada's 1958 Citizen of the Year," the Springhill survivor topped the list of 21 nominees with 51 percent of the vote. The January 22, 1959 edition of the *Telegram* anointed Ruddick as "an inspiration to his companions in their nine-day entombment before miraculous rescue came." He returned from the *Telegram* awards ceremony (where Ontario Premier Leslie M. Frost paid tribute to his courage) so buoyed up he appeared, in Greene's vivid description, "dazed with happiness."

Ruddick returned to Springhill and faced new and unexpected personal challenges. Some townsfolk prized the recognition awarded their hometown folk hero, but many others, including his co-workers, were baffled, resentful and felt slighted by the praise heaped upon him in the immediate aftermath. The smoldering resentment erupted in fits of disgust over one miner being singled out in a town where nearly every family experienced personal loss.

Ruddick's fame quickly disappeared and he faced a difficult road ahead. The mine closed and, like most of his mine buddies, he could not find work. When his unemployment insurance ran out, Maurice and his family of 15 barely survived on the allowance cheques and the measly disaster relief payments of $88 per month and $35 per week.

The man tagged as "the Springhill hero" struggled and his life went downhill. Ruddick formed a musical troupe with his children, the Harmony Babes, and toured the Maritimes singing country songs. Toward the end of his life, spent mostly in a lonely existence, he was reduced to gathering loose coal from the abandoned mines and the nearby railway tracks to heat his house and keep his family from freezing during the winter.

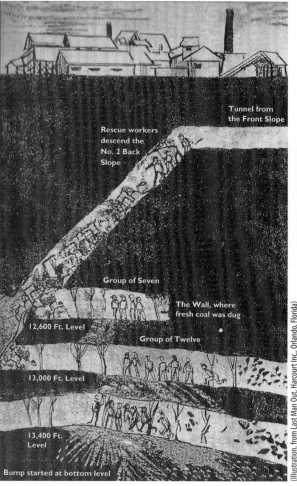

(Illustration, from Last Man Out, Harcourt Inc, Orlando, Florida)

(Top) Inside North America's Deepest Coal Mine: An artist's rendering of Springhill Mine No. 2 at the time of the Disaster, October 23, 1958. The Bump started at the bottom and trapped miners at various levels below ground, essentially isolating the two groups who were the last to be rescued.

The story of Nova Scotia's coal industry after Springhill did not have a happy ending either. Coal still hangs like "a black residue" over much of former mining communities in Cumberland, Pictou, Inverness and Cape Breton counties. Memories of those days linger on lives lived in the former company houses and become more visible the closer one looks at what remains of the "coal black heart" of Nova Scotia.

Mining some five-hundred million tons of coal under often terrible underground conditions took its toll in terms of lives from the early years up until 1969. It's estimated that about 2,500 men — more than Nova Scotia lost in the First World War — perished in those mines, a death rate far higher than in the mines of modern China. Hundreds of others died a slower death, victims of emphysema, cancers and heart ailments contracted during a working life in the pit. Halifax's John DeMont, raised in a Cape Breton mining family, found something below the surface in his interviews with surviving miners, a certain "poetry in their lives." "God knows," he once said, "life was hard, but there was this immense endurance, and epic ability to put one foot down in front of the other and kind of soldier on."

Digging Deeper – For Further Reading

Brown, Roger David, Blood on the Coal: The Story of the Springhill Mining Disasters. Windsor, NS: Lancelot Press, 1976.

DeMont, John, Coal Black Heart: The Story of Coal and the Lives it Ruled. Toronto: Doubleday Canada, 2009.

Greene, Melissa Faye, Last Man Out: The Story of the Springhill Mine Disaster. Orlando, Florida: Harcourt Inc., 2003.

McKay, Cheryl, Spirit of Springhill: miners, wives, widows, rescuers and their children tell true stories of Springhill's coal mining disasters. Los Angeles, CA: Purple PenWorks, 2014.

Nova Scotia Archives, Men in the Mines: A History of Mining Activity in Nova Scotia, 1720-1992. Online Archives at novascotia.ca/archives/meninmines/capebreton.asp

Turning Point 9

The Robert Stanfield Era:
Modernization of Nova Scotia, 1956-1967

Flying into Halifax on an airplane from anywhere in the world, the point of arrival is Robert Stanfield International Airport. That regional airport bears the name of one of Nova Scotia's most revered premiers and a man widely regarded as "the best Prime Minister Canada never had."

With the passage of time, Robert Stanfield's Nova Scotia legacy has faded and he's now best known as the federal Progressive Conservative leader from 1967 to 1976, who narrowly lost the 1972 federal election to the Liberal giant Pierre Trudeau. It's often forgotten that, as Premier of Nova Scotia (1956 to 1967), Stanfield ushered in what his campaign appeal called "The New Nova Scotia."

Robert Lorne Stanfield, born in Truro on April 11, 1914, may well have been the most modest, unassuming and civil public figure in 20th-century Canada. That unique persona was captured well in Geoffrey Stevens' classic 1973 biography entitled simply *Stanfield*. Glimpses of his unique personality are evident in Dalton Camp's fascinating 1970 memoir, *Gentlemen Players and Politicians*, including priceless firsthand accounts of his experiences campaigning with Stanfield in Nova Scotia in the 1950s.

TRURO FAMILY TRADITION

Born and raised in a prominent Truro family famous for producing Stanfield's underwear, Robert Stanfield was a remarkably private gentleman imbued with a sense of *noblese oblige*.

(E.D. Haliburton, Lancelot Press)

(Left) The Stanfield Cabinet. Premier Robert Stanfield and his cabinet, 1956. Left to right: Clifford Levy, Layton Fergusson, "Ned" Manson, E. D. Haliburton, G. I. (Ike) Smith, Robert Stanfield, Mac Leonard, R. A. Donahue, and Steven Pyke. Premier Stanfield chaired the cabinet and also served as Education Minister.

"A fortunate origin and background allowed him not to need to scramble for financial success," as Richard Clippingdale aptly stated, then added: "A fine brain made him enormously observant and thoughtful. Public service — bureaucratic, political and governmental — was the life he was made for and gladly chose."

After what he described as a "normal upbringing" in the Colchester County hub town, young Robert was whisked off in Grade 11 to Ottawa, where he attended the exclusive boys' school Ashbury College. Mixing with the sons of the rich did not suit him, but it was here that he felt the first stirrings of a social conscience.

The greatest influence on his intellectual journey was Professor Russell Maxwell, his economics instructor at Dalhousie University. He was initially stumped by Maxwell's Socratic method of teaching, then came to thrive under his tutelage. When he graduated with his B.A. in Economics from Dalhousie in the spring of 1936, he did so with the Governor General's Gold Medal for the graduating student with the highest overall academic standing.

KEPT HIS HEAD DOWN

During his four years at Harvard University in Boston, Stanfield hit the books, kept his head down, listening to classical music on his portable Magnavox phonograph record player. Former boarding house roommate Philip Elman was stunned, years later, to discover that he had entered politics. His law school friend, he recalled, shunned drinking parties, avoided confrontations and never uttered "an unkind word or mean thing about anyone."

Stanfield was also something of a homing pigeon. Upon graduating from Harvard Law School, he shunned attractive American job offers and headed back to Nova Scotia to enter law practice.

"He wanted to come back to Canada," Maxwell said. "This was his plan for his life." That route led, almost inevitably, to provincial politics, where he was welcomed with open arms by the long out-of-power Conservative Party of Nova Scotia.

Toronto advertising man Dalton Camp, a New Brunswick-born political organizer dispatched to Nova Scotia in the 1950s to help Stanfield's Conservatives win election, found the Tory leader to be a mighty peculiar political animal.

Encountering Robert Stanfield for the first time in 1953, in the law office of McInnes and Stanfield at 156 ½ Hollis Street, Camp confronted a person described to him as "a dull, dour man." His vivid description of Stanfield bears repeating. "Well, I thought, at least he's not pretty. Long-headed, with shrewd, heavily lidded eyes…, a long nose, and full mouth. All else was elbows and knees. He invited me to sit down and for a while there was an uneasy silence."

The Conservative leader knew he faced long odds campaigning against Nova Scotia Liberal premier and political titan Angus L. MacDonald. When asked by Camp about his prospects, Stanfield hesitated and replied in a voice with "depth and resonance … 'Oh, I don't know. We don't expect to win, but we expect to do better. (Pause) Somewhat.'"

Stanfield lost the 1953 provincial election, but the Stanfield Team candidates gained a foothold in the Legislative Assembly. Three years later, facing MacDonald's successor, Henry L. Hicks in the September 1956 election , Stanfield won 23 seats, the Liberals 19, and the Cooperative Commonwealth Federation (CCF) one — marking the end of a 23-year Liberal dynasty.

'NEW NOVA SCOTIA'

A 42 years of age, Robert Stanfield became Canada's youngest premier up to that time. His campaign for a "New Nova Scotia" was considered an upset and Toronto Tories like Dalton Camp and George Drew saw it as a "national omen" of better times ahead.

Upon his election, Stanfield and his Conservative government faced enormous economic challenges. Post-war Canadian development in the critical sectors of industry, transportation, and technology had largely by-passed Nova Scotia. Coal still dominated the economy, employing 7,500 workers, but was becoming increasingly obsolete, costly to mine and difficult to transport. The mines were only kept open with massive federal subsidies.

Steel was Nova Scotia's second largest employer, but the early warning signs were present. Cape Breton was heavily dependent upon Dominion Steel and Coal Company, which employed 4,000 people, and stood as the largest employer east of Quebec. With coal production falling, the province's industrial base was shrinking.

Nova Scotia's shaky economy made New York's big financial underwriters nervous and Stanfield was advised that the province's A credit rating was threatened. "We felt," Stanfield later said, "that we had to run very hard just to stand still." Everywhere Stanfield and his cabinet looked — in agriculture, fishing, forestry and coal mining — some reorganization was needed to solidify the provincial economy.

OVERDUE CHANGES

Stanfield's first government was remarkably activist introducing modernizing changes that were both small and far-reaching. With the staunch support of his chief lieutenant G.I. (Ike) Smith, the Premier ushered in a number of overdue changes: introducing provincial hospital insurance, increasing funding for poor relief and asylums for the "harmless insane," improving miners' pensions, raising the ceiling on farm loans, and creating new work restoring the fortress at Louisbourg.

Premier Stanfield's major initiatives proved to be lasting contributions. He established Nova Scotia's first provincial parks, subsidized the building of a large livestock abattoir and appointed the first independent auditor general, responsible to the Legislature and significantly improving public accountability. In spite of public skepticism, he moved, in 1962, to establish an office of economic planning to alert the province to economic trends and produce forecasts, identifying, in its 1965 report, the critical need for job creation.

Stanfield's biggest policy legacy was in the promotion of industrial and resource development. Upon achieving office, he resumed negotiations, started by the Hicks government, to secure a giant pulp mill for Port Hawkesbury on the Strait of Canso. He revived the project with the Swedish industrial combine Stora Kopparbergs Bergslags A.B. Utilizing a Canadian subsidiary, Nova Scotia Pulp and Paper Ltd., Stora Kopparbergs worked with the Stanfield government to build a $40-million bleached sulphite pulp mill five kilometres south of Port Hawkesbury. That mill, by 1973, employed hundreds with a $10-million annual payroll, and was eventually regarded as Stanfield's greatest development success.

NEW TERRITORY

In his first session as premier, Stanfield ventured into new territory by proposing a Nova Scotia Industrial Corporation, a unique development institution, funded by the province, but also supported by selling public shares. It was aimed to confront, head on, the fundamental issue of industrial decline and the hemorrhaging of young people to other, more affluent provinces. "The problem was," biographer Stevens pointed out, "that there was no way the development corporation, if it were to be effective, could expect to pay a return on the shareholders' investment. Profits had to take second place to the creation of jobs."

In the fall of 1957, Stanfield replaced his initial legislation, after receiving clear feedback from the Nova Scotia supermarket tycoon Frank Sobey and other leading businessmen. In its place, the Stanfield government established Industrial Estates Limited (IEL), a wholly owned Crown corporation backed by $12 million in government funds.

The key figure in IEL was Sobey, its unsalaried president who served in that capacity until 1969. Although Stanfield's industry minister sat on the IEL board, the development agency was given great latitude in attracting industries with a whole range of government incentives and subsidies. It started out as a lender of funds but ended up being more of an active partner in new industrial ventures.

After attracting a small textile plant to Stellarton, IEL stepped up its operations. A whole string of other companies followed, some medium-sized, but most of them relatively small, at the rate of five or six new plants a year.

Eventually, bigger companies took advantage of IE L and its incentives: National Sea Products in Lunenburg, General Instruments, in Sydney, Canada Cement in Brookfield and Crossley-Karastan Carpet Mills in Stanfield's hometown of Truro. Some risky investments did not pay off and IEL was forced to intervene with the odd bailout.

(Bob Ball, Canadian Press)

(Top) Fumbling the Football, 1974: During the decisive 1974 federal election, while waiting to refuel his plane in North Bay, Ont., Stanfield passed the time by tossing around a football with ease. In a sad twist of fate, it was Stanfield's one fumble that landed on the front page of *The Globe and Mail* - and quite possibly cost him the election.

(Canadian Press)

(Top) A Thoughtful and Dignified Leader: An official photo of Robert Stanfield as he appeared in 1974 running against the flashy Prime Minister Pierre Trudeau.

Two giant automobile product manufactures were attracted to Nova Scotia and considered the Stanfield government's biggest successes in industrial development. Volvo (Canada) Limited was attracted to Dartmouth, and, at its height of operations, rolled out 230 cars a week. Canadian Motor Industries, based in Sydney, operated a small plant, which assembled Japanese-made Toyota cars.

The biggest catch was the French tire maker, Michelin, which produced 1,500 jobs in New Glasgow, Pictou County. That contract, negotiated by Stanfield, came to fruition after he had left for Ottawa.

'STANFIELD'S VIETNAM'

Today IEL is also remembered as "Stanfield's Vietnam," an industrial development project with well-publicized disasters. Attracting the Toronto-based stereo and television producer Clairtone to Nova Scotia was a major higher risk venture and it ended in disappointment. The IEL role in bringing Deuterium Canada Ltd., a "Heavy Water" project to Cape Breton, proved to be a bigger embarrassment.

Stanfield knew that his government was gambling when he established IEL to bring industries to Nova Scotia. He was also mindful of the province's critical need for new sources of prosperity and employment. The sad sagas of Clairtone and the DCL heavy water plant demonstrated what can happen when a government, with the best of intentions, tries to do too much, too quickly, without enough due diligence.

The Clairtone and heavy water projects proved to be bubbles that went bust. Instead of transforming Nova Scotia into a North American capital of stereo systems and colour television, Clairtone swallowed up $20 million in subsidies and left behind a vacant seven-acre factory in Stellarton. Pledging to build a $30 million heavy water plant on Cape Breton Island, Deuterium of Canada cost the province $130 million over 10 years and left behind a rusting plant in Glace Bay. Explaining away the disasters, Tory strategist Camp commented that "the reach exceeded the grasp."

'PROGRESSIVE' TENDENCIES

Such industrial misadventures failed to dent Stanfield's sterling reputation. Premier Stanfield epitomized the Conservative with distinct "progressive" tendencies. His initial cabinet was small, numbering eight, and the government was relatively lean, befitting his sound conservative values. Unlike many Nova Scotia Conservatives, including some of his own cabinet, he was not inclined toward preserving the status quo. As his agriculture minister, Ed Haliburton wrote: "Stanfield is the kind of leader who can adapt to changing situations. He is not doctrinaire, nor dogmatic, his ideas are not rooted in the past."

Premier Stanfield also embraced a Nova Scotia First philosophy. In the summer of 1966, the giant Bell Telephone Company with assets of $2.7 billion made an offer to acquire 51 percent of the shares of Nova Scotia's locally owned Maritime Telegraph and Telephone Company with

NATIONAL PC LEADERSHIP CONTEST

July 20, 1967: Premier Stanfield denies—oops, pardon me —announces his candidacy for the National PC leadership.

(Robert Chambers, Herald Archives)

assets of $114 million. With the spirited editorial support of *The Chronicle Herald*, Stanfield stepped in with legislation to ensure MT&T remained under Nova Scotia control. From then on, according to then NDP leader James Aitchison, Stanfield could "do no wrong."

Stanfield's call for a "New Nova Scotia," got him elected, but his upstanding character and forthright manner won him repeated re-election. Modest and pensive by nature, he conveyed an image of quiet strength, dignity and resolve. There was, Stevens noted, a "private inner core" that even those who knew him well could rarely penetrate. Even though he lived in the Halifax South End, he walked almost daily to his office at the Legislative Assembly and made a point of eating dinner with his wife and children.

ON TO OTTWA

Premier Stanfield did not look ambitious, so when he decided to seek the federal Progressive Conservative Party leadership in May 1967, that move caught even political junkies off guard. He only yielded to the pressure to run after winning over his closest ally Ike Smith and securing a pledge from him to carry on the Stanfield Conservative agenda in Nova Scotia.

With the federal Conservative Party under the 71-year-old John G. (The Chief) Diefenbaker fending off "termites" from within, the party voted in November 1966 for a leadership review.

The Chief vowed to defend his leadership at a rousing national leadership convention on September 9, 1967, at Toronto's Maple Leaf Gardens. Diefenbaker fought doggedly but in vain to retain the leadership. When the smoke cleared, Stanfield had won the convention endurance test, defeating Manitoba premier Duff Roblin on the fifth ballot to become Leader of the Official Opposition PC's in Ottawa.

Under Stanfield, the federal Conservatives solidified their political hold on Nova Scotia and Atlantic Canada, resisting the nationwide tide of "Trudeaumania" in June 1968 that brought Pierre Trudeau and the Liberals to power. As Opposition Leader in Ottawa, Stanfield fought gamely against the charismatic Liberal Prime Minister and presided over a remaking of Progressive Conservative policy to give the party a more modern appeal. Working with Trent University president Thomas H. B. Symons, the Stanfield-led party adopted a more reformist edge, including a policy plank calling for progressive tax reform and the introduction of a guaranteed income for Canadians struggling below the poverty line.

Robert Stanfield came within a whisker of toppling Trudeau in the close October 30, 1972 federal election, losing by just two seats. In the final tally the Liberals won 109 seats and the Conservatives 107. Stanfield served with steadfast purpose and rare integrity for four more years, up against a reawakened Liberal government.

(Right) Saving Maritime Telegraph and Telephone, 1966: Premier Stanfield stepped in to thwarted Bell Telephone's plan to acquire a controlling interest in the local telephone utility.

(Robert Chambers, Herald Archives)

'THE TORY SYNDROME'

Like previous Conservative leaders, Stanfield faced internal party divisions as the party struggled to shed what Queen's University political scientist George Perlin called "the Tory syndrome." As a federal opposition party, long out of power, the Stanfield PC party remained riddled with factionalism and rife with contrarians.

From 1967 until 1976, Stanfield had to contend with internal resistance from an aggrieved Diefenbaker and his rump group. Without any significant party support in Quebec, Stanfield promoted a conciliatory "deux nations" policy and fended off a backlash from his Western Canadian caucus members opposed to Trudeau's expansion of official bilingualism. He paid a heavy price for his conciliatory policy on bilingualism and Quebec recognition.

Stanfield was the complete antithesis of Pierre Trudeau and a rather formal, dignified and unexciting politician who was up against a vibrant and dazzling contemporary. In one telling exchange, after Trudeau reversed his position and introduced wage and price controls, political pundits and cartoonists had a field day making fun of Stanfield's reaction with images of "Zap, you're frozen." In his otherwise lightweight 1973 *Memoirs*, Trudeau paid sincere tribute to Stanfield as "an opponent I liked and respected … He was intelligent and reflective, not aggressive." Times had changed and it was Trudeau, not Stanfield who represented the spirit of the age.

There were, in short, two Robert Stanfield's: the reform-minded, steady provincial PC premier revered by Nova Scotians and the methodical, gentlemanly federal Opposition leader who was no match for Trudeau I (the First).

Digging Deeper – for Further Reading

Camp, Dalton, *Gentlemen, Players and Politicians*. Toronto: McClelland and Stewart, 1970.

Clippingdale, Richard, *Robert Stanfield's Canada: Perspectives on the Best Prime Minister We Never Had*. Kingston, ON: McGill-Queen's University Press, 2008.

Haliburton, E. D., *My Years with Stanfield*. Windsor, NS: Lancelot Press, 1972.

McMillan, Tom, "Robert Stanfield and Tom Symons," in Ralph Heintzman, ed., *Tom Symons: A Canadian Life*. Ottawa: University of Ottawa Press. 2011, chapter 6.

Perlin, George C., *The Tory Syndrome: Leadership Politics in the Progressive Conservative Party*. Montreal and Kingston: McGill-Queen's University, 1980.

Stevens, Geoffrey, *Stanfield*. Toronto: McClelland and Stewart, 1973

Turning Point 10

The Razing of Africville:
A Failed Urban Renewal Project, 1962-2010

"Welcome to Africville" read the sign at the north end of Barrington Street, where the pavement ended and a dirt road began. Down the road, former resident Charles R. Saunders recalled in *The Spirit of Africville* (1992), was a special, protective, out-of-sight place you could call home.

Yet Africville was, to most Haligonians, 'the other side of the tracks,' and a collection of ramshackle, run-down wooden houses beside the city dump, bordering the Bedford Basin. To civic leaders in the 1950s, it was considered a ghetto and a blot on Halifax's reputation as a modern city. The vast majority of citizens, as Caribbean-born Nova Scotian teacher and lawyer Gus Wedderburn put it, "never saw the flowers."

Africville was once the best known Black or African-Canadian community in Canada. A whole host of national and international documentaries, books, magazine articles, television and radio programs, poetry and songs have all popularized the story of the destruction of that small North End, African-Nova Scotian community.

A CRITICAL TURNING POINT

Bulldozed out of existence in the late 1960s, Africville was a critical turning point in Halifax race relations. That tragedy did not completely erase Africville, which remains the spiritual home of the African-Nova Scotian community and a source of strength in the continuing struggle against segregation and racism in Atlantic Canada.

The Africville story is often cited as a glaring example of racism in action. Since the appearance of Jennifer Nelson's 2008 book, *The Razing of Africville*, that's been the dominant narrative.

(Bob Brooks, Archives of Nova Scootia/PANS)

(Left) Fetching Water in Africville: Without city services, local residents obtained water from wells marked with Boil Water signs.

Such a perspective is rather narrow because the whole Africville saga was much more than a Black and white racial clash.

While recognizing plenty of evidence of racist motivations, some more recent studies of Africville's demise see it as a more complex and multifaceted urban relocation project gone seriously awry. One of the earliest academic Africville researchers, T Dalhousie sociologist Donald Clairmont, sees the uprooting of Africville as the result of three factors converging in the late 1950s and 1960s: overt and hidden racism, the progressive impulse in favour of racial integration and the rise of liberal-bureaucratic social reconstruction ideas.

Drawing upon the groundbreaking work of American scholar James C. Scott, two prominent historians, Tina Loo and Ronald Rudin, have cast the relocation as a tragic example of a "muscular ideology" termed "high modernism" that vested complete faith in state "social engineering" and "scientific knowledge" to remake entire communities and landscapes.

Rudin, in particular, sees clear parallels between Africville dissolution and other massive post-war state projects, such as the relocation of Eastern Ontario communities to make way for the St. Lawrence Seaway and the obliteration of Ste-Scholastique for Mirabel Airport northwest of Montreal.

HIDDEN RACISM

Concordia urban geographer Ted Rutland contends, in his 2018 book, *Displacing Blackness*, that the removal of Africville was a prime example of the hidden racialized agenda of urban planning. "Displacing blackness" was the unwritten modus operandi of municipal planning as an instrument of power and race. Remaking downtowns exemplified racialized thinking because it left neighbourhoods like Africville "racially cleansed" and suitable for transforming into "places of enjoyment" and gentrified housing. .

Africville in the 1950s was an almost entirely African-Nova Scotian community located on the northern fringe of Halifax, fronting the Bedford Basin. Established in the 1840s, it was a sadly neglected, almost rural community numbering about 400 in the mid-1960s, when it was designated for urban redevelopment.

The catalyst for the radical change was a 1957 report, *A Redevelopment Study of Halifax*, prepared by architect Gordon Stephenson, a member of the "high modernist" school of design thinking. Africville, in Stephenson's eyes, was a blot on the city's reputation. Stung by his claim that Africvlle "stands as an indictment of society and not its inhabitants," city officials used "relocation" as a means of ridding Halifax of one of its "blighted" areas and trying to improve the material conditions of its inhabitants.

Halifax City Council in the 1950s considered the issue to be the "Africville Problem." By 1956, the city's population had reached 93,000 and the expanding metropolitan area had added 60,000 people between 1945 and 1956. The city proper on the Halifax Peninsula was considered pushed to its limits. Council was preoccupied with glaring housing problems and attracted to urban renewal projects, mostly funded by federal and provincial governments.

(Right) Daily Life in Africville: A Mother beckons children for dinner.

(Bob Brooks, Archives of Nova Scotia/PANS)

COMPLETE RELOCATION

The Stephenson report identified the value of the Africville land for industrial and harbour development. In 1961, council's Housing Policy Review Committee recommended clearance of existing housing in Africville. Since most of the Africvillians were reluctant to vacate their ancestral lands, complete relocation on an individual basis was deemed the only viable approach.

Large-scale housing projects were underway in the north and central districts of the city, reasonably close to Africville. A large public housing complex, Mulgrave Park, built to house the many urban poor, mostly low-income Black and white families, was seen as part of the solution.

The relocation of Africville was considered just a small piece of the overall urban renewal plan. Given the small size of the North End community, it represented only about 10 percent of the number of people being relocated in the city.

City planners and building engineers were fully committed to the "high modernism" of "slum clearance." Like modernizers in other cities, they placed a priority on upgrading housing stock and urban beautification, not the needs of the uprooted residents.

A July 1962 Halifax Development Department report estimated the cost of acquisition and clearance of Africville property at between $40,000 and $90,000. Displaced residents were to be offered alternative housing in unsegregated, subsidized rental housing. Those without "legal title" to their plot of land were promised $500.00 in compensation. Any disputes over compensation would be decided by negotiation and ultimately the courts.

'HISTORICAL INJUSTICES'

The relocation scheme had serious shortcomings. "There was nothing in this plan," Donald Clairmont once wrote, "about the historical injustices, nothing about the community life and nothing about new opportunities for the people."

A surprising number of progressive thinkers supported the relocation of Africville. One of them was Alan Borovoy, then a young Toronto lawyer and later revered as Canada's undisputed champion of civil liberties.

In August of 1962, Borovoy travelled from Toronto to Halifax for four days and, acting as a community organizer, helped to form the Halifax Human Rights Advisory Committee (HHRAC), committed to promoting racial integration and assisting the Africvillians in securing equality rights and better housing.

Borovoy, like Stephenson, showed little appreciation for Africville's traditions and saw the enclave as an example of the legacy of racial segregation. He stated flatly that a "black ghetto should not be subsidized" and strongly advocated racial integration in what he saw as a divided city.

Without appreciating the social solidarity of Africville, the outspoken Toronto lawyer viewed the African-Nova Scotian community in the context of a much wider struggle for civil rights in Nova Scotia and elsewhere in North America. Years later, Borovoy remained surprisingly unrepentant about his role, pointing out that the community had few viable options, given the absence, at the time, of much in the way of local community organization.

Once the HHRAC appeared on the scene, it became the almost exclusive channel to be used in City-Africville contact and negotiations regarding relocation and related issues. Only one formal meeting of Africville residents was held outside HHRAC auspices. It happened in October 1962, when Reverend William Pearly Oliver convened a meeting of 30 Africville residents in Seaview Baptist Church.

(Right) Appealing for Racial Integration: Toronto lawyer Alan Borovoy addresses Seaview Church meeting, August 1962.

Sponsored by the Nova Scotia Association for the Advancement of Coloured People (NSAACP), Reverend Oliver's gathering discussed the relocation question and concluded, however reluctantly, that under the circumstances, relocation was inevitable and therefore the focus should be on negotiating the best terms possible.

A SPLIT COMMUNITY

The Africville community was split over the impending relocation. At a large public meeting held in August 1962 most, if not all, Africvillians present rejected the city's plans to relocate them, but given the odds stacked against the community a smaller faction grouped around Rev. Oliver gradually came to accept the inevitability of their community's relocation.

Throughout the autumn of 1962 and the whole of 1963, the HHRAC attempted to broker a deal with Africville residents to smooth the way for relocation. Working with a handful of African Nova Scotians, only three of whom were from Africville, the committee concluded that bringing the Africville houses up to "city specifications" would cost some $800,000 and was cost prohibitive and morally unacceptable because it perpetuated segregation.

To override Africville resistance, city council called in a leading expert, Dr. Albert Rose, a University of Toronto specialist in the field of housing, urban renewal and social welfare. After one meeting with the HHRAC and only two hours touring the community in late November 1963, Rose weighed in on the "Africville situation." Fresh from Toronto where the Regent Park Plan of urban redevelopment was considered *avant guard*, he found Africville conditions deplorable, rehabilitation too costly and segregation morally indefensible.

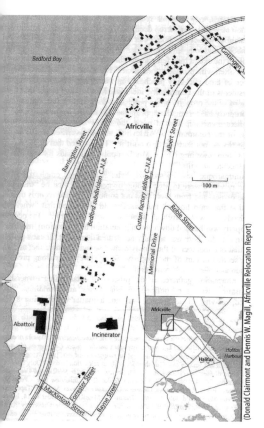

(Donald Clairmont and Dennis W. Magill, Africville Relocation Report)

(Top) The Africville Community, Africville Area Plan, City of Halifax, 1962.

APPALLING NEGLECT

As an outsider, Rose was appalled by the neglect of, and conditions in, Africville. Surveying the landscape, he saw Africville as a blighted area crisscrossed with railway tracks and occupied and surrounded by a prison, two hospitals for infectious diseases, an incinerator, a few "dirty" factories, two slaughterhouses and a garbage dump. Without city water or sewage services, Africville residents used local wells and water had to be boiled to avoid contamination from hospital runoff containing traces of infectious germs.

Rose's report, delivered a few weeks later, broke the back of resistance. He found the residents of Africville "ready and eager to negotiate" and convinced that, if it had been a white community, it would have been cleared a long time ago. In January 1964, after favourable press coverage, the HHRAC and an Africville community gathering voted to accept the report. In short order, Halifax City Council unanimously accepted the Rose report and set up a special committee to oversee the clearance of Africville.

The actual relocation took place over three years between 1964 and 1967. Guided by a hired social worker, the plan proceeded "house to house" until the settlement was cleared of residents. The first deal in 1964 involved a willing woman who sold her house (without land title) and received $500.00, free moving, accommodation in public housing and cancellation of an outstanding $1,500 hospital bill.

City expenditures far exceeded the initial $70,000 estimate for relocation and eventually reached some $800,000, roughly equal to the projected cost of redeveloping Africville housing. The trustees of Seaview Church accepted an offer of $15,000 for their church building and used the proceeds to establish an education trust fund, designed to assist children of the Africville relocatees.

DISPOSSESSION

The relocation plan focused almost exclusively on removing Africville residents with no follow up in 1968 to assess its impact on families. One member of the HHRAC, supportive of the plan, realized too late that the displaced were "just left completely to their own resources."

"I should have known," he said, "but I didn't." What started out as a relocation, ended up being a dispersal of Africville's inhabitants.

Holdouts remained when the city social worker's contract ran out in 1967. Construction of the base for the new MacKay Bridge forced the issue and brought an end to the imposed relocation. In December 1969, facing expropriation threats and intimidation, the last Africville resident, Aaron "Pa" Carvery, was summoned to City Hall, offered a take-it-or-leave-it cash payment and presented with an ultimatum. Finally, on January 2, 1970, Carvery relented and signed away his property. Four days after he vacated the premises, his house was bulldozed.

90 - TURNING POINTS

Digging Deeper – for Further Reading

Africville Genealogical Society, The Spirit of Africville. Halifax: Format Publishing, 1992.

Clairmont, Donald H. and Dennis William Magill, Africville: the life and death of a Canadian black community. Third Edition. Toronto: McClelland and Stewart, 1974.

Loo, Tina, "Africville and the Dynamics of State Power in Postwar Canada, Acadiensis, Vol. XXXIX, No. 2 (Summer/Autumn 2010), pp. 23-47.

Nelson, Jennifer J., Razing Africville: a geography of racism. Toronto: University of Toronto Press, 2009.

Rutland, Ted, Displacing Blackness: Planning, Power and Race in 20th Century Halifax. Toronto: University of Toronto Press, 2018.

Tattrie, Jon, The Hermit of Africville: The Life of Eddie Carvery. Lawrencetown Beach, NS: Pottersfield Press, 2010.

The Carverys of Africville continue to be among the best known former residents. When the bulldozers came to raze his home, Irvine Carvery was just 15 years of age, but he recalls the early days fondly. After falling down on a broken bottle and cutting his hand while playing with friend Terry Dixon, he went to the nearest house and was immediately patched up by that neighbour. It illustrated, for him, the sense of community and "the closeness and the oneness of the people."

AN APOLOGY

As President of the Africville Genealogy Society, Carvery, a former Chair of the Halifax Regional School Board, played an instrumental role in securing official redress for the grave injustice. Forty years after the relocation, in February 2010, a City Council headed by Mayor Peter Kelly issued an apology and pledged $3 million to build a replica church and cultural centre.

Little remained of Africville when Mayor Kelly spoke to a crowd of 250 at the North End YMCA, except a small park designated a national historic site in 2006. "Words cannot undo what has been done," Kelly said. "But we are profoundly sorry and apologize to each and every one of you ..."

One of those who interrupted Mayor Kelly shouting "Give it back!" "Compensation!" and "You forgot the people!" was Irvine's brother, Eddie Carvery, now immortalized in Jon Tattrie's 2010 book, *The Hermit of Africville*. After trying his luck at a succession of occupations, from community organizer to sheet metal worker to fisherman, he had returned to the ruins of Africville in 1970 to start a protest of his own, pitching a tent, then living in a small trailer, across from the site in a dog park called Seaview. Forty years after the razing of Africville, he continues his lonely vigil in a struggle for survival with the faint hope for justice.

Most Nova Scotians in the 1960s sided with the modernizers and were essentially blind to the unseen beauty of Africville. Prominent lawyer and Black educator Gus Wedderburn, who initially supported relocation, only came later to recognize the razing of Africville inflicted deeper wounds in terms of social costs. Holding up a faded photograph of the community in the 1991 film, *Remember Africville*, he says in sad tones, "I did not see the flowers ... I did not see the flowers."

That is the real lesson of Africville.

Turning Point 11

The Savage Revolution:
The Perils of Reinventing Government, 1993-1996

For four tumultuous years — 1993 to 1997 — the traditional political order of Nova Scotia was turned on its head. The Liberal government of Dr. John Savage challenged many of the established ways in public life and took a serious stab at "reinventing government" and improving the responsiveness of public services.

The "Savage Years" in Nova Scotia politics were a short-lived period of intense reform, but tremendously significant in many ways. The four-year period, as depicted in a 2000 collection of essays entitled *The Savage Years*, was a "distinct political era" when Savage's administration "broke sharply with many entrenched ways of governing" and, in spite of being short lived, left behind a lasting legislative legacy.

The election of the Savage administration disrupted what was, up until the 1980s, a rather conventional two-party system characterized by what the late Dalhousie political scientist J. Murray Beck described as "traditionalism and conservatism." Changes in party rule, he wrote, required "conditions" that were "altogether catastrophic in nature." Like Tweedledee and Tweedledum, the two parties "continue to exist, because they have existed." And in Lord James Bryce's compelling depiction: "The mill has been constructed and its machinery goes on turning, even when there is no grist to grind."

(Top) Transition Meeting, June 1993: Incoming premier John Savage sits with the former PC Premier Don Cameron whom he defeated in the May 1993 provincial election.

'NEO-LIBERAL ERA'

Looking back more recently, St. Francis Xavier University political scientist Peter Clancy now sees the Savage interregnum as providing Nova Scotia with a rough transition to the so-called "neo-liberal era" of budget tightening and public-sector wage restraint. It also marked, as Mount St. Vincent University professor Jeffrey MacLeod has shown, a failed attempt to end party patronage and curb "clientism" in the public policy domain.

With the benefit of more hindsight, the Savage Liberals look to Clancy more like a "crisis management brigade" of public-services reformers than a conservative-leaning administration committed to cutting programs and reducing the footprint of government.

Premier John Patrick Savage broke the mould as a Nova Scotia politician. The son of an Irish doctor with a Welsh Baptist wife, he was born a Catholic in Newport, Monmouthshire, Wales, on May 13, 1932. After graduating from Queen's University, Belfast, and training at the Newport hospital, he became a family physician and served with the Royal Army Medical Corps on troop ships.

Dr. Savage settled down to become a GP in Magor, Monmouthshire, with his wife Margaret and six young children. As a family physician, he began to speak out against the National Health Service and emerged as a well-known critic of the UK healthcare system.

When Nova Scotia placed an advertisement in the *British Medical Journal*, Savage answered the call and moved in 1967 to join a medical practice in Dartmouth, NS. He started Dartmouth programs for drug addicts and promoted sex education in the schools, bringing him into conflict with local Catholic priests. After growing a beard and opening a clinic for Black families in East Preston in the late 1960s and early 1970s, he was dubbed in the press as "the Hippie Doctor."

He started his political career in the 1970s as a Dartmouth school board member, ran twice unsuccessfully as a federal Liberal candidate and was elected Mayor of Dartmouth in 1985. While mayor, he championed the development of Alderney Landing and actively supported cultural causes, most notably the Dartmouth Book Awards.

(Left) N.S. Premier John Savage, Queen Elizabeth, and Dartmouth Mayor Gloria McCluskey, 1994.

PROVINCIAL LEADERSHIP

When the provincial Liberal Party ran into leadership difficulties in in the winter of 1992, Mayor Savage was recruited to run for the leadership, which he won on the second ballot against four candidates, in a telephone-in vote, in June 1992.

With Savage as leader in the May 1993 provincial election, the Nova Scotia Liberals led the public opinion polls and ran a safe campaign promising "more jobs" for Nova Scotians. Giving little hint of what was to come, the Savage Liberals swept into power, defeating sitting Conservative premier Donald Cameron and winning 40 of the legislature's 53 seats.

Premier Savage took office determined to do politics differently. What he inherited was a full-blown fiscal crisis. Nova Scotia had yet to recover from a serious 1990-1992 recession and the forecasted budget deficit for 1992-93 stood at a staggering $600-million without adding other costs such as crown corporation loses, pension fund obligations or workers' compensation.

FINANCIAL CRISIS

Newly installed Minister of Finance Bernie Boudreau advised the Premier that the province was facing a "major financial crisis" with no choice but to act to rein in public expenditures. Bad news reigned over Savage and his new cabinet as "every day" Boudreau and his officials "turned over a new rock." Cape Breton's major employer, Sydney Steel, was also on the financial rocks, and the entire Sysco board resigned *en masse* as word leaked out that the company's credit lines were completely exhausted.

Savage and his cabinet were driven more by the financial exigencies than by any ideological convictions. Their first priority was to put the province's financial house in order and to achieve a balanced budget over four years. They were also committed to re-engineering government itself to deliver improved and more accountable public services.

While Savage's approach has been compared to that of more conservative provincial counterparts, including Sterling Lyon of Manitoba's rock-ribbed conservatism, Ralph Kline of Alberta's harsh austerity, and Mike Harris of Ontario's "Common Sense Revolution," that comparison is mostly off the mark. Unlike his contemporaries, he sought to rehabilitate the province and brought a doctor's perspective to the job of curing what ailed government services.

The new Nova Scotia premier was also a political bird of a different stripe. He was socially progressive by nature with a reputation in Dartmouth for embracing social causes and pioneering new forms of medical treatment. As a genuine independent thinker, he also harboured a visceral dislike of traditional party patronage and favourtism as well as a positive outlook on the potential of the public sector for doing good and acting as an economic and social stabilizer.

Savage fashioned a cabinet with a seven-member inner circle assigned to the key departments: Finance, Education, Health, Economic Development and Municipal Affairs. Finance Minister Boudreau chaired a Priorities and Planning Committee integrating overall policy-setting with

(Joseph Robichaud Photography/ Halifax City Archives, Dartmouth Collection)

(Top) Alderney Gate Sod Turning Ceremony: Mayor John P. Savage and Joseph Zatzman perform ceremonial duties to initiate the redevelopment of the Dartmouth ferry terminal site, December 7, 1988.

the provincial budget process. The core cabinet members, including Savage, were heavily influenced in their thinking by David Osborne and Ted Gaebler's *Reinventing Government* (1993), the most influential public policy reform tract of the time.

Imbued with a Nova Scotian variation of that public management reform zeal, Premier Savage and Boudreau made a clean break with past practice and replaced most, if not all of the holdover deputy ministers and senior advisors. Early on in their mandate, they realized that changing the culture might exact a political price. Acting together as a "critical mass in cabinet," the core bloc of ministers was, in Boudreau's words, "prepared to decide matters in the provincial interest and (to) place political considerations second."

(Left) Policy Reversal, 1993-1994: *The Chronicle Herald's* Bruce Mackinnon takes direct aim at Dr. John Savage for campaigning for "more jobs" and then "chopping" jobs in the public sector.

(The Chronicle Herald Archives)

REFORM AGENDA

The crushing budget problem weighed heavily on the Savage inner circle and they came to see themselves as trustees of a broad provincial restructuring and reform agenda. Putting the financial house in order was first on that agenda and it came early in their mandate.

The Budget Speech on September 30, 1993 revealed just how serious the Savage cabinet was in reining in the deficit. It promised $75 million in program-expenditure cuts for the 1993-1994 fiscal year, and a total of $300 million in cuts to be spread out over four years. Taxes and user fees were raised, civil service salaries rolled back and the numbers of public-service positions scaled back. Public service staff reductions were to be achieved through attrition and early retirement incentives but the Finance Minister refused to rule out layoffs to achieve the target staffing levels.

The strong budget medicine came out of nowhere for most Nova Scotians. A new, more determined and technocratic John Savage emerged in the Premier's Office. While he campaigned in the 1993 election to create jobs and limit budget cuts to $180 million, that promise fell by the wayside in the wake of the "fiscal crisis." Costlier, in political terms, was being forced to abandon his promise not to raise provincial taxes.

Savage and his core cabinet managed to ride out the budget storm during their first year and to demonstrate a surprising capacity to manage fiscal restraint effectively. That left Savage in a paradoxical position, as a hard-nosed, cost-cutting premier who was actually a small "l" liberal with a demonstrable social conscience. Lost in the maelstrom caused by the budget reductions was Savage's deeper commitment to preserve the long-term capacity of the province to deliver improved public services and social programs after quickly correcting the perilous state of provincial finances.

A TALENTED CABINET

The Premier fell short in selling his governmental reform agenda to the public. The Dartmouth doctor was more of a pragmatist than a natural politician. As mayor, he was regarded as a big spender but prided himself in "never giving anyone a job."

Although successful at the municipal level, Savage spoke with a reedy voice and traces of Welsh and Irish intonation in his speech. He was not, by his own admission, a political animal and found it difficult to establish an easy rapport with voters. While calling upon Nova Scotians to tighten their belts, he attempted to eliminate or curtail political patronage, a secret potion normally used to grease the wheels of the party in power. That combination spelled political trouble for his government.

Savage's cabinet was loaded with capable and resourceful ministers. His Minister of Education, John MacEachern, a former Glace Bay high school math and physics teacher, emerged as one of the Savage government's most energetic and articulate policy advocates. He won over Education Department officials and they responded by producing a creative spurt of educational change proposals, including school-based management and governing councils.

During 1994, MacEachern survived a severe test, achieving cost efficiencies by raising class sizes and improving public accountability by introducing school-level governance. When provincial bargaining with the Nova Scotia Teachers Union reached a stalemate, the Minister stood his ground. After several weeks of what Peter Clancy described as "brinkmanship," a teachers' contract agreement was finally reached in early June 1994, one that strengthened to province's hand on the education front.

Cabinet colleague Dr. Ron Stewart, a North Sydney raised physician renowned for his emergency medicine innovations in Los Angeles and Pittsburgh, tackled the job of Health Minister with the fervour and courage of a healthcare reformer. He made it clear from the outset that comprehensive health service restructuring was in the offing. As a rookie MLA from Cape Breton and a newly appointed minister, Stewart faced an entrenched bureaucracy that he was never able to tame or manage, in spite of his undeniable talents.

RESTRUCTURING HEALTHCARE

Dr. Stewart's tangle with Nova Scotia's healthcare portfolio carried real life lessons. Restructuring the healthcare system was a formidable undertaking and one that took its toll. The professional healthcare groups, ranging from doctors to nurses to para-professionals, proved uncooperative, and the serious issues afflicting healthcare provoked emotionally charged clashes. After three years, Stewart resigned, seemingly defeated by the beast aptly described by his successor Boudreau as "the line department," so enormous and difficult to manage that "all others pale into insignificance."

One cabinet minister who survived the Savage years was Deputy Premier Bill Gillis, a veteran Antigonish MLA first elected in 1970. The former geology professor at St. Francis Xavier University exercised a moderating influence in cabinet. Little in his personality or inclinations was radical at all, but his reading of small-town Nova Scotia values tended to serve as a counterweight to the more mission-oriented ministers.

The Savage government could point to a series of lasting legislative achievements. Bringing the provincial budget under control and withstanding the tsunami of organized opposition was their biggest accomplishment. Lesser known, but no less significant, were the Savage administration's measures aimed at reinventing public-sector management and service delivery at the local level.

PUBLIC SECTOR REFORM

Under Premier Savage, the education system was reformed, strengthening regional school boards and establishing school-level advisory councils. Confronting aging school buildings and a major construction backlog, the deficit-ridden Savage government took the plunge into public-private partnerships (P3s) to finance and meet the pent-up demand for new schools.

Working with four private developers — the Hardman Group, Nova Learning, Scotia Learning and Ashford Investments — the province leveraged private capital and enterprise to build at first six schools, then another 33, all over a five-year period. Far more public schools were built, adhering to high quality standards, but the scheme proved politically unpopular, particularly in public sector union households.

Governmental reform extended to many areas. Service delivery in the healthcare system was improved through the creation of more publicly accountable regional health authorities. Nova Scotia also acquired its first province-wide ambulance and paramedic service and a whole network of regional development agencies. Embracing the concept of regional government and brushing aside public resistance, local municipalities in Nova Scotia's two metropolitan areas, Halifax and Sydney, were amalgamated into regional municipalities.

The Savage years represent a pivotal turning point in Nova Scotia public life because a one-term government left its mark by ushering in a particular form of neo-liberal politics unique to Nova Scotia. The rather staid political culture of the province was clearly unprepared for the Liberal program of public sector restructuring and reform.

Digging Deeper – for Further Reading

Adamson, Agar and Ian Stewart, "Party Politics in the Not So Mysterious East," In Hugh Thorburn, ed, Party Politics in Canada. Scarborough, ON: Prentice Hall, 1996.

Beck, J. Murray, "The Party System in Nova Scotia: Tradition and Conservatism," in Martin Robin, ed., Canadian Provincial Politics. Scarborough: Prentice Hall, 1972, pp. 168-197.

Clancy, Peter, James Bickerton, Rodney Haddow, and Ian Stewart, eds, The Savage Years: The Perils of Reinventing Government in Nova Scotia. Halifax: Formac Publishing, 2000.

Clancy, Peter, "Nova Scotia: Fiscal Crisis and Party System Transition," in Bryan M. Evans and Charles E. Smith, eds., Transforming Provincial Politics: The Political Economy of Canada's Provinces and Territories in the Neoliberal Era. Toronto: University of Toronto Press, 2015, pp. 77-109.

MacLeod, Jeffrey, "Nova Scotia Politics: Clientism and John Savage," Canadian Journal of Political Science, Vol. 39, No. 3 (September 2006), pp. 553-570.

(Left) Premier Savage Under Fire, 1995: A close-up of Premier Savage shows the stress and strain of staying the course in the "Savage Revolution."

(The Chronicle Herald Archives)

John Savage's time in office ended rather abruptly and that tended to obscure the remarkable and lasting legacy his government left behind. The Premier, by his own admission, was less than convincing in selling his reform agenda, and his incredibly talented band of ministers were reformers who knew that they may end up as a one-term government. His campaign to eradicate party patronage bred dissent within the Nova Scotia Liberal Party, forcing Savage to face a leadership review in July of 1995. By March of 1997, the party forces were gathering again, and Savage resigned as Premier. A memorable Toronto Globe and Mail editorial on March 22, 1997, identified Savage's list of reforms, called him "the best premier in a generation" and chastised Liberal party members and the public for hounding him out of office.

The Savage Revolution created more than its share of disruptive innovation, but it tended to spook the provincial Liberal Party. While Savage hoped to see his program carried on, traditionalists recaptured the party and chose a rather conventional federal Liberal backbencher Russell MacLellan as his successor. The affable Cape Bretoner was not one to challenge established practices and spent his brief two-year tenure attempting to undo the more contentious measures of the Savage reform program.

The Savage Years can now be assessed in the round and in relation to political change over the past two decades. Dr. John Savage's government stands out as perhaps the most productive, yet controversial, in the province's history.

The Savage Revolution brought a unique brand of neo-liberalism to Nova Scotia — a governmental philosophy sympathetic to the activist state, conscious of bureaucratic intransigence and dedicated to 'reinventing' public services to serve people better. It also galvanized social democratic forces and solidified public-sector workers, strengthening their ties with an emergent New Democratic Party movement. That political realignment would come to shatter the traditional two-party system and help smooth the way for a future NDP government.

Indigenous Communities in Nova Scotia

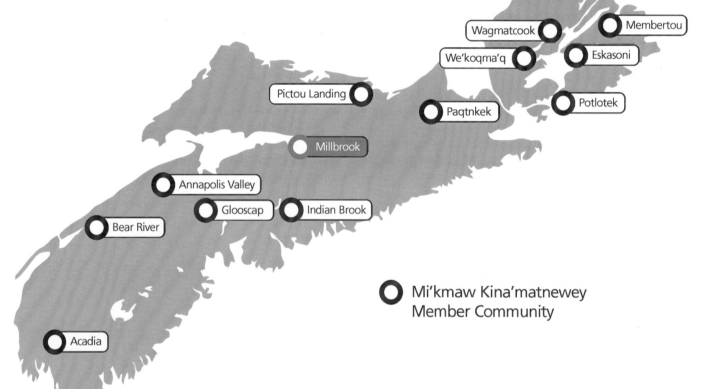

Wagmatcook

Membertou

We'koqma'q

Eskasoni

Pictou Landing

Paqtnkek

Potlotek

Millbrook

Annapolis Valley

Glooscap

Indian Brook

Bear River

Acadia

Mi'kmaw Kina'matnewey Member Community

Turning Point 12

Educational Self-Determination:
Creation of the Mi'kmaw Kina'matnewey, 1997-2012

The Nova Scotia Mi'kmaq have emerged since the 1990s in the forefront of the national movement for Indigenous control over education. Almost 40 years ago, a Mi'kmaw band-operated school opened on Chapel Island, now known as Potlotek, offering the first Mi'kmaw- English bilingual education program. Out of that initiative at Mi'kmawey School emerged the kernel of the idea of establishing Indigenous schools run by Mi'kmaq communities, aggregated together in their own community school system.

The dream of a Mi'kmaw network of schools came to fruition in 1997 as the *Mi'kmaw Kina'matnewey* (MK), a First Nation education authority managed by the Mi'kmaq and funded by the federal Department of Aboriginal Affairs and Northern Development. Today's MK schools, operating in 12 of the province's 13 Mi'kmaw communities, may be small and enroll only 3,000 students, but it offers distinctly Mi'kmaw school programs and has significantly raised graduation rates for Indigenous students.

Graduating from high school continues to be out of reach for far too many Indigenous students, in province-after-province, right across Canada. While the proportion of Canadian on-reserve adults under the age of 25 with a high school diploma barely rose (from 25 to 30 percent) from 1996 to 2006, Atlantic Canada bucked that trend, rising from 55 percent to 65 percent. By 2012-13, some 88 percent of Grade 12 students in MK schools completed their graduation year.

(Photo: Mi'kmaw Kina'matnewey)

ENORMOUS POTENTIAL

(Below) First Nations Roundtable, Dalhousie University, 2016. Chief Morley Googoo represented the Mi'Kmaq on the panel Left-to-right: Chief Googoo, Patti Doyle-Bedwell, Richard Florizone and Indigenous Affairs Minister Carolyn Bennett help set the stage for the roundtable.

Within the Mi'kmaw band schools, graduation rates tend to be inflated because they are based upon Grade 12 completion rates rather than the proportion of students entering Grade 9 or 10 who secure a high school diploma. Even so, the rise in academic attainment levels is real and a clear sign of the enormous potential of Indigenous-run community schools to change students' educational outcomes and life chances.

(Top) A group of Mi'Kmaw students at an Art Show

(Dalhousie University/ Nick Pearce photo)

The recent success of Mi'kmaw schools has not gone unnoticed. One prominent Mi'kmaw Chief, Morley Googoo, trumpeted that success as Chair of the Education Committee for the National Assembly of First Nations (AFN). Former Toronto *Globe and Mail* Education reporter Jennifer Lewington looked closely at the Mi'kmaw model in a 2012 article in *Education Canada* and observed that Mi'kmaw student success was "winning national attention as a possible model for First Nation self-governance in education."

(Opposite) Success Story: Karlee Johnston, a grade 12 student at Chief Allison Bernard Memorial High School in Eskasoni, and a member of the first graduating class of the province's first Mi'kmaq Immersion Program

INDIGENOUS CONTROL OF EDUCATION

The educational governance of Indigenous peoples in Canada has long been the preserve of federal government authorities. The British North America Act of 1867, and later the Constitutional Act of 1982, established a dual system of education in Canada, designating provincial authority over education, but retaining federal responsibility for Indian education. Conflict has arisen over the "collision of educational practices and differing world views" held by a succession of "White Man's" governments and Indigenous peoples in Canada.

The Indian Act effectively institutionalized the exclusion of Indigenous communities, Elders and parents in the delivery of educational services. In spite of repeated attempts, reforms to the Indian Act, most recently in 1985, have not significantly changed the governance framework. With the 2015 election of the Justin Trudeau government, the promises made have not only injected fresh hope but also whet the public appetite for real change.

Since the 1972 National Indian Brotherhood (NIB) paper *Indian Control of Indian Education*, Indigenous people in Canada have been seeking greater local control over education, more parental involvement in educational decision-making affecting children and more support for the promotion of Indigenous languages and culture. Some progress has been made because, as the Senate Committee on Aboriginal Affairs noted in 2011, "parental responsibility and local control of on-reserve education is much more prevalent today." The creation of the Mi'kmaw education authority and the expansion of Mi'kmaw-run schools contributed to that breakthrough in parent and community participation in the schools.

A Group Photo of MK students, taken in February of 2014.

(MK, http://kinu.ca/)

Digging Deeper – for Further Reading

Aboriginal Affairs and Northern Development Canada. Summative Evaluation of the Elementary/Secondary Education Program on Reserve, Final Report. Ottawa: Government of Canada, June 2012.

Battiste, Marie. Decolonizing Education: Nourishing the Learning Spirit. Saskatoon, SK: Purich Publishing, 2013, pp. 87-93.

Lewington, Jennifer, "In Nova Scotia, A Mi'kmaw Model for First Nation Education." Education Canada, Theme Issue, 2012. Toronto: Canadian Education Association, 2012, pp. 14-15.

Mi'kmaw Kina'matnewey, Return of Education Jurisdiction to the Mi'kmaq. Sydney, NS: Membertou First Nation, 2013.

Mi'kmaw Kina'matnewey, "An A+ for Mi'kmaq Education," February 24, 2014. Sydney, NS: Membertou First Nation, 2014.

Paquette, Jerry and Gerald Fallon, First Nations Education Policy in Canada: Progress or Gridlock? Toronto: University of Toronto Press, 2010.

One area of great concern to Indigenous communities is how the Canadian government and the provinces define "achievement." Indigenous Elders and scholars espouse a different conception of achievement much broader than strictly book learning. If we draw on the insights from the First Nations Holistic Lifelong Learning Model — advocated by First Nations scholar Marie Battiste — teachers, principals, parents, families and communities are all mentors and nurturing guides responsible for their children's achievement in all aspects of learning.

THE TALKING CIRCLE

School is part of a lifelong learning journey for children and youth. It is not a quantifiable journey in that Indigenous learners are often both Indigenous and modern — and draw wisdom and insights from both dominant Canadian and Indigenous perspectives and knowledge bases. The principle and practice of local school-based decision making, for example, would be greatly enhanced by the adoption of the "Talking Circle" tradition in Mi'kmaw culture and spirituality.

The Nova Scotia Mi'kmaw model may well represent a viable option for breaking what Indian Act experts Jerry Paquette and Gerald Fallon aptly termed the "gridlock" in Indigenous governance. In 1997, nine Mi'kmaw chiefs and the Minister of Indian Affairs Ronald Irwin secured a consensus, after five years of negotiations, and signed An Agreement with Respect to Mi'kmaw Education Nova Scotia. Subsequent provincial and federal legislation enabled the Mi'kmaq to opt out of the Indian Act and gain jurisdiction over primary, elementary and secondary educational programs and services.

Two years after the agreement, the Mi'kmaw Education Act became Canadian law, eventually bringing 11 of 13 Mi'kmaw communities under that umbrella and recognizing the right to local decision making on educational curriculum including language, history, identity and customs. Under the Self-Governing Arrangement (SGA), schooling is now provided to some 3,000 students in 12 Mi'kmaw communities.

The Nova Scotia Mi'kmaw education model is what one seasoned Indigenous education observer described as "an overnight sensation" that was 20 years in the making. It is the culmination of two decades of experience in building the Mi'kmaw Kina'matnewey, an Indigenous education authority which, in 2012, provides overall coordination, professional services and $40 million in federal monies to community schools. Most significantly, the three party (federal, Indigenous and provincial) agreement recognizes the role of the education authority to support local band schools in delivering language immersion and other culturally based programs and activities.

Early indications are that students are more engaged because of pedagogy and curriculum more attuned to Mi'kmaw traditions. In 2010-11, the Mi'kmaw Kina'matnewey reported rising high school graduation rates much more competitive with the province as a whole. That success rate impressed Scott Haldane, chair of a 2012 federal First Nations governance review panel, and demonstrated the potential benefits of extending to Indigenous communities elsewhere more autonomy in managing their own community schools.

The Orange Crush:
The Rise and Collapse of Nova Scotia's First NDP Government, 2009-2013

On June 10, 2009, the bold morning headline in The *Chronicle Herald* read "Orange Crush." The lead story celebrated the smashing victory of Darrell Dexter's New Democratic Party and heralded the arrival of Nova Scotia's first NDP government.

Dexter's NDP secured power by toppling the Rodney Macdonald-led Progressive Conservatives and winning a 31-seat majority in the 52-seat House of Assembly. That historic Orange Crush breakthrough government lasted only four years.

Former NDP MLA Howard Epstein provided the most trenchant commentary on what happened: like the orange-coloured soft drink, the NDP in power proved to be sugary to the taste but lacking in nourishing qualities. The Dexter government also committed a few political blunders.

'AMORPHOUS SIMPLICITY'

The NDP was elected on what St. Francis Xavier University professor Peter Clancy aptly described as "an electoral platform of amorphous simplicity under the slogan 'Darrell Dexter: For Today's Families.'" It was also perfectly in tune with Dexter, a Dartmouth lawyer-turned-politician who personified a pragmatic "conservative progressive" approach to politics and favoured incrementalist policies over the ideological pursuit of big ideas.

The 2009 NDP platform, fashioned by Dexter and his inner circle dominated by NDP master strategist Dan O'Connor, made only seven commitments: to create jobs in all sectors; keep emergency rooms open and reduce healthcare wait times; help young people stay in the province; remove the harmonized sales tax (HST) from home energy; fix rural roads; help seniors stay in their homes and live within our financial means by controlling deficits.

Since its inception in the 1930s, the social democratic party known as the Co-operative Commonwealth Federation (CCF/NDP) has wrestled with an internal dilemma. "Socialists belong to movements, capitalists support parties" is how UBC political scientist Walter D. Young put it back in 1969. Since then, any public claim to being "democratic socialists" engaged in a political movement has been dropped in favour of what Desmond Morton termed the social democratic "dream of power."

Dexter inherited a political apparatus that was clearly more of a "party seeking election" than a democratic socialist movement hot in pursuit of a better, more just world. From 1968 until 1980, Cape Bretoner Jeremy Akerman had built a spunky, rough and ready Nova Scotia NDP that was more pragmatic than doctrinaire.

Together with fellow Cape Bretoner Paul MacEwan, Akerman succeeded in breaking the political ice and electing two MLAs in 1970, three in 1974 and four in 1978. While building the party he tangled often with a more ideological Halifax-based faction and came to despise what MacEwan described as "the purist mentality" of his Halifax enemies.

(Communications Nova Scotia)

(Left) Delivering the 'Back to Balance' Budget: Finance Minister Graham Steele presents the April 6, 2010 budget raising the HST from 13 to 15 per cent, breaking an election promise.

"I'm ambidextrous -- with my left hand, I toss bouquets with my right hand and I point the finger of scorn."

(Robert Chambers/The Chronicle Herald Archives)

OUT OF THE POLITICAL WILDERNESS

Akerman's successor, NDP Leader Alexa McDonough, the well-heeled daughter of Shaw Bricks founder Lloyd Shaw, first elected as MLA for Halifax Chebucto in 1981, led the party out of the political wilderness. Starting out as the lone NDP member and only woman in the House, she shed her image as a limousine socialist, bridged the two competing factions and fought tirelessly for progressive causes.

Unlike McDonough, Darrell Dexter was in most respects a regular Nova Scotian. Born September 10, 1957, he was the son of Elvin, a steel metal worker, and Florence Dexter (née Pace), and grew up in the rural community of Milton, near Liverpool on the South Shore. He was the first member of his family to go to university and cut his political teeth as a volunteer in the 1979 McDonough federal election campaign.

After acquiring Dalhousie University and King's College degrees in education and journalism, Dexter worked as a reporter for the *Halifax Daily News* in the early 1980s, then served in the Canadian Navy as a sub-lieutenant and combat information officer on board HMCS *Yukon* and HMCS *Qu'Appelle* while deployed with Maritime Forces Pacific. Following his tour of duty, he became a practicing lawyer.

Dexter worked his way up in politics. He was first elected as a Dartmouth city councillor, serving from 1994 to 1996, then was elected to the Nova Scotia Legislature as MLA for Dartmouth-Cole Harbour in 1998. Sitting in the Opposition under NDP leaders Robert Chisholm and Helen MacDonald, he proved reliable as the critic for economic development and health, and was re-elected with ease in 1999, 2003 and 2006.

BREAD-AND-BUTTER ISSUES

The NDP "Class of 1998" consisted of six elected MLAs who mirrored the party's traditional divisions by representing both the party faction and the movement faction. As Cole Harbour MLA, Dexter emerged as a common-sense politician focusing on bread-and-butter issues, while the Halifax Chebucto MLA, Howard Epstein, was far more explicit about his philosophical commitment to democratic reform, environmentalism and social justice.

Dexter emerged triumphant in the NDP provincial leadership contest held in June 2001 at McNally Hall, Saint Mary's University. Following the party's meteoric rise under the attractive and appealing Chisholm and the short MacDonald tenure, party members settled for a steady hand and a known quantity.

One of the party's brighter political lights, Halifax-Fairview MLA Graham Steele, had this to say in his 2014 bestselling political memoir, *What I Learned About Politics*, about why he supported Dexter for leader: "He was not charismatic or bold, but rather safe and solid, which are harder qualities to sell the public. But he was my kind of New Democrat, and I definitely didn't want the other faction to take control of the party."

His counterpart in the other faction, Epstein, saw Dexter through a completely different lens. In his 2015 memoir *Rise Again: Nova Scotia's NDP on the Rocks*, he explains why he was rankled by Dexter's favourite expression, often repeated: "There's no DNA test for belonging to the NDP."

Serving under Dexter, he chafed at leadership that eschewed what he defined as "core traditional worldviews" aligned with labour rather than business, and the reluctance to occupy "an identifiable place on the political spectrum."

Ten days after the 2009 election, Premier Dexter unveiled the first NDP cabinet in Nova Scotia's history. All six original members of the caucus were given cabinet posts, except for Howard Epstein. It was a stunning rebuke to the de facto standard-bearer for the progressive, activist wing of the party. Close Epstein friend and ally Christopher Majka, a rabble.ca reporter, saw it as sending a clearer signal to the movement faction that they would "have no voice at the cabinet table."

Future NDP leader Rev. Gary Burrill, the MLA for Colchester-Musquodoboit Valley from 2009 to 2013, received similar treatment at the hands of Dexter and his loyalists. Close political observers also detected little social democracy or labourism in the NDP program.

BACK TO BALANCE

Finance Minister Graham Steele's budget consultations, labelled Back to Balance, fresh into the mandate, made it abundantly clear that the Dexter government was fully committed to achieving a balanced budget within four years. The premier's professed admiration for Manitoba Premier Gary Doer's Tony Blair-inspired policy agenda seemed to telegraph that his government would be offering little more than "a humane version of neo-liberalism."

If Nova Scotians elected the NDP expecting a different brand of politics or a change in direction, their hopes were going to be disappointed. The Dexter government was inclined to play it safe by focusing on addressing a specific, rather narrow, set of social concerns. Fearful of attack from business and the public for their supposed "socialist" leanings, they came more and more, according to Peter Clancy, to resemble a continuation of the "neo-liberal" era initiated by the John Savage administration.

(Right) The Swell of Victory: Premier-elect Darrell Dexter waves to supporters at NDP election night headquarters at the Dartmouth Holiday Inn on June 9, 2009.

(TIM KRCCHAK / Herald Staff)

With Steele's Back to Balance initiative underway, Saint Mary's University professor Larry Haiven delivered a stinging critique of the Dexter government's commitment to slaying the deficit. His well-timed 2009 policy paper, entitled "The Sky is Falling, The Sky is Falling, or Is It?" connected the dots between Dexter's approach to deficit reduction and that of Saskatchewan NDP Finance Minister Janice MacKinnon, fully explained in her 2003 book *Minding the Public Purse*.

Boxed in by promising balanced budgets, Haiven saw the Dexter NDP emulating Saskatchewan in commissioning an audit to expose a "fiscal crisis" and using that report to "kill expectations" of reformers committed to genuine social democratic initiatives.

The leading faction of the Dexter NDP was certainly well versed in the established practices of politics. Like the Liberal and PC governments before them, the Dexter administration adhered to what Graham Steele has termed the Rules of the Game:

- Nothing is more important than getting elected and re-elected;
- Focus on voters' beliefs, not the facts;
- Keep everything as simple as possible;
- Keep everything as secret as possible;
- Fight for influence and status;
- Always be loyal to your party and leader;
- Always attack other parties;
- Take credit often and avoid blame always;
- Focus on constituency work;
- Deny these are the rules.

Few Nova Scotians well versed on politics and attuned to Dexter's NDP in power would be surprised by this list. It reflected a deep skepticism that would not normally be associated with a truly social democratic reform movement.

DEFICIT REDUCTION

Irrespective of the overarching political mode of operations, Dexter's NDP government from 2009-13 did move the policy yardsticks in a few critical areas. Under Finance Minister Steele, the province confronted the impact of the 2008-09 recession and provided responsible fiscal management while offshore revenues were declining and Ottawa was adjusting the equalization formula in ways that posed budget challenges. Through it all, the NDP managed to move the province closer to balancing the budget, increasing Nova Scotia's credit rating and lowering the debt to GDP ratio from 48.7 percent to 36.6 percent.

Environment, energy and climate change were assigned a much higher priority. The Dexter government placed hard caps on greenhouse gas emissions (GHGs); announced very enterprising renewable energy targets of 40 percent by 2020; made significant investments in renewable energy, particularly in wind and hydro; inaugurated a solid program of renewable energy feed-in tariffs; made significant progress on energy conservation through Efficiency Nova Scotia; banned uranium mining; initiated a province-wide review of hydraulic fracturing, extended the moratorium on gas and oil drilling on Georges Bank and acted on the province's commitment to increase protected lands from 12 percent to 13 percent.

Confronted with the collapse of Bowater Mersey's pulp and paper plant in Dexter's former hometown of Liverpool, the government took the hit and came up with an innovative policy solution, supporting the Buy Back the Mersey program. It succeeded in bringing 225,000 hectares of working forest and woodlands under public management and supporting a community forest initiative to practice sustainable harvesting and help to stimulate rural revitalization.

POLITICAL DAMAGE

Cancelling the Yarmouth CAT ferry service without providing time to readjust or any alternative turned out to be an epic disaster. While visitors from the United States by ferry had declined from 40,000 in 2006 to 23,000 in 2009, the ferry service provided an anchor for the tourist industry of Southwest Nova Scotia, a district without much economic activity beyond seafood fishing. It was, as Epstein stated succinctly, an early decision, driven by provincial financial concerns, that was "indicative of inexperience, haste, misplaced priorities, and stubbornness" that inflicted political damage in that region and far beyond.

The honeymoon normally accorded an incoming government came to an end on February 3, 2010, the day Auditor General Jacques Lapointe released his explosive report on MLA expenses. Every detail in the AG's report dealt with expenses incurred before the NDP was elected into power. Yet it unfolded under Premier Dexter's watch and he was slow in recognizing the damage being inflicted on all politicians. It also stuck in Finance Minister Steele's craw because he had been alerting his NDP colleagues to the potential for controversy for a decade or more.

The daily revelations of MLA expense irregularities, covered extensively in *The Chronicle Herald* and on CBC News, eventually touched the premier when a few questionable expenses came to light, including the payment of his lawyer's fees. For a politician with a deserved reputation for standing up for the little guy, his defensive responses left a bad impression.

Whether it set in motion the downward slide to Dexter's personal "political destruction," as Steele claimed, is debatable when so many factors came into play in his fall from grace. Early "Back to Balance" education cuts and successive waves of rural school closures caused political woes for NDP Education Minister Ramona Jennex. The former Grade 1 teacher and provincial teachers' union representative found herself defending education cuts that aroused NSTU president Alexis Allen and resulted in a very public call for her resignation.

Dexter stood by Jennex and did his best to ignore well-financed media ad campaigns with provocative messages that ranged from "Kids Not Cuts" to "Cut to the Core." Liberal Leader Stephen McNeil and his education critics were effective in cozying up to the NSTU and burying the memories of the Savage era in teacher-government relations.

(Left) Salmon Feedlot Protest, 2013: The Dexter NDP government's $25-million grant to Cook Acqaculture became a lightening rod and protesters claimed that the NDP was behind the spread of salmon fish farms.

ALIENATING THE CORE

After taking a laissez-faire approach to school closures, Jennex finally weighed in with a provincial moratorium in early April 2012, too late to recover lost ground in rural Nova Scotia. A late-term spending spree failed to alter the widespread perceptions among teachers about NDP education initiatives. Education, in Epstein's rather terse assessment, was "not well-handled" under the Dexter NDP.

Most damaging was the Dexter NDP's strained relations with hardcore supporters and environmental activists. On June 24, 2012, Dexter and his NDP caucus members received a shocking letter, prepared by educator Molly Hurd and her partner, Dalhousie economics professor Lars Osberg, and signed by 50 Halifax NDPers associated with the movement faction of the party. The letter, reprinted in Epstein's memoir, contended that the NDP under Dexter had lost its way and drifted far from its social democratic foundations. Hurd, Osberg and the signatories expressed concern over the government's budget priorities, spelled out as:

- Give (via forgivable loan) $304 million to the Irvings;
- Cut the tax rate for large corporations;
- Forced spending cuts on healthcare and primary, secondary and post-secondary education.

While acknowledging that "the government must pay its bills," the NDP faction expressed deep disappointment that their hopes for a government committed to "values of social justice" had been dashed. Attempts to bring the two sides together, brokered by south-end Halifax cabinet minister Leonard Preyra, were to no avail. The damage had been done and Dexter loyalists dismissed the group as a posse of Haligonians "living within five blocks of one another."

UPHILL BATTLE

The 2013 NDP campaign for re-election was an uphill battle against public opinion that had coalesced around the Liberal Opposition led by the physically towering Annapolis MLA Stephen McNeil. Through the clever and skillful use of media and television commercials during 2013, the Liberal campaign brain trust had successfully targeted the Nova Scotia Power monopoly and fashioned a folksy, down-home image of the Liberal leader. It was possible to conceive of Stephen McNeil standing up for Nova Scotians and clearing away obstacles in the way of local enterprise.

Governments tend to defeat themselves and it happened once again. Dexter and his government were in bad odour with most of the core interests that dominate Nova Scotia politics, particularly local business chambers, the teachers' union and environmental advocacy groups. It's never a good sign when NDP candidates encounter a multitude of signs calling out their poor record on shelling out millions for a Halifax convention centre, subsidizing the Irving Shipyard, approving expanded salmon-lot farms and cutting education to the bone.

Dexter's NDP government came crashing down on election day, October 8, 2013. The Orange Crush was over and a so-called "red tide" had swept McNeil's Liberals into power with 33 seats and some 45.4 percent of the popular vote. Dexter's party was reduced to a rump of seven seats and the premier himself was narrowly defeated in Dartmouth-Cole Harbour.

In one of the great ironies of Nova Scotia politics, former NDP Finance Minister Graham Steele, who did so much to shape the NDP government's economic agenda, was as cool as a cucumber on election night 2013, providing informed, dispassionate commentary on the CBC-TV News coverage of the disaster. It was another lesson in the peculiar vagaries of politics.

Digging Deeper – for Further Reading

- *Epstein, Howard, Rise Again: Nova Scotia's NDP on the Rocks. Halifax: Empty Mirrors Press, 2015.*

- *Haiven, Larry, "The Sky is Falling, The Sky is Falling, or Is It?" Canadian Centre for Policy Alternatives Discussion Paper. Halifax: CCPA, 2009.*

- *MacEwan, Paul. The Akerman Years: Jeremy Ackerman and the Nova Scotia NDP 1965-1980. Antigonish, NS: Formac Publishing, 1980.*

- *Steele, Graham, What I Learned About Politics: Inside the Rise and Collapse of Nova Scotia's NDP Government. Halifax: Nimbus Publishing, 2014.*

- *Young, Walter D., The Anatomy of a Party: The National CCF 1932-1961. Toronto: University of Toronto Press, 1969.*

Daniel N. Paul

WE WERE NOT
THE SAVAGES

A Mi'kmaq Perspective on the Collision between
European and Native American Civilizations
NEW Twenty-First-Century Edition

(Fernwood Publishing)

Turning Point 14

The Cornwallis Controversy:
Daniel Paul, We Were Not the Savages, and the Toppling of a Monument, 1993-2018

For more than 25 years, a public controversy raged over the public commemoration of the first Halifax-based Governor of Nova Scotia, Edward Cornwallis, recognized for generations as the founder of Halifax.

The polarized debate revolved around two strongly held opinions. For many Haligonians, Cornwallis was the city's founder who laid the foundations for colonial Nova Scotia. To others, he was the epitome of British "settler colonialism" and a "genocidal imperialist" whose claim to notoriety was placing a bounty on the scalps of the Indigenous inhabitants of *Mi'kmak'ki*, the ancestral home of the Mi'kmaq people.

The fundamental question came down to this: should Cornwallis continue to be honoured with a public statue in downtown Halifax, or should all public marks of his existence —monuments, places and streets — be removed from public view? That debate was so intense that it generated more letters to Nova Scotia's daily newspaper, *The Chronicle Herald*, than any other issue over a span of two decades. It also captured national attention as a test case in the larger public debate over who we honour from our nation's past.

The Cornwallis controversy can be traced back to the 1993 publication of a much-debated popular history book, *We Were Not the Savages*, researched and written by Daniel N. Paul, a widely respected Mi'kmaw Elder and social justice advocate. It effectively filled in the gaps in the story of the Mi'kmaq from the beginnings to their fateful clash with Governor Cornwallis and subsequent European colonizers.

THE SCALP PROCLAMATION

The critical piece of evidence unearthed by Paul was the Governor's September 30, 1749 proclamation placing a price on the head of all Mi'kmaw men, women and children, in retaliation for a raid on a group of English settlers occupying land outside of the Halifax fortifications on the Dartmouth side across the harbour from Halifax. The Mi'kmaq, Paul pointed out, responded with a similar proclamation, but it applied only to British soldiers and in unceded ancestral lands being occupied by the colonizers. The scalp proclamation, in Paul's book, is highlighted as a prime example of how the British incited horrible acts of human carnage and scuttled any hope for peace in British settler-Mi'kmaq relations.

When *We Were Not the Savages* appeared, it attracted immediate attention and sparked fierce debate. Nova Scotia Premier John Savage not only attended the book launch, but spoke at the event and encouraged dozens of prominent people to join him in the audience. "It's time," Savage said, "for history to be presented how it transpired."

The ensuing debate centred on Governor Cornwallis and his reputation, not only in Nova Scotia, but in his brutal military campaigns against the Scots. It turned on repeated tales of his rather unappealing character and imperialist attitudes that raised the question of whether he deserved to be honoured in public places.

Paul wrote the book to restore pride in Mi'kmaw history and traditions as well as to tell another side of the story of Nova Scotia's early colonial experience. Prior to his book, it was common for public figures and historians to exalt British traditions and deny the brutalities inflicted by Europeans on the colony's first inhabitants, the Mi'kmaq.

The author saw the book as an opportunity to rally the Mi'kmaq people and to enlist the support of Haligonians outraged by Cornwallis' actions and the impact of white settler-colonialism on the fate of Indigenous people far beyond Nova Scotia. Between 1993 and 2017, Paul's book sold 50,000 copies and ranks among the most read Nova Scotian advocacy books of all time.

DEEPLY DIVIDED

The Cornwallis debate left Haligonians and Nova Scotians deeply divided with little middle ground. Defenders of the Cornwallis legacy held fast to the claim that he deserved official recognition as the founder of Halifax who laid the early foundations for British settlement, governance, law and the courts. Fierce opponents sided with Paul and castigated Cornwallis for his elitism, imperialist views and barbaric treatment of not only the Mi'kmaq but also the Acadians and the Scots.

Daniel Paul and his supporters continued to champion the cause of erasing Cornwallis' presence from the public square. With the support of the Confederacy of the Mainland Mi'kmaq, he continued to advocate for social justice and an end to racial discrimination. For his tireless work, Paul was honoured himself with an Order of Canada and an Order of Nova Scotia.

Public opinion favoured preserving Cornwallis' statute and a very active group known as the Military Heritage Preservation Society, spearheaded by Leo Deveau, John Boileau and Len Canfield enjoyed some success. Provincial polling surveys conducted by Corporate Research Associates showed that a majority supported keeping the statue in Cornwallis Park. Halifax writer John Tattrie, author of *Cornwallis: The Violent Birth of Halifax* (2013), learned, firsthand, what it was like to walk across the minefield of controversy.

The whole debate gradually began to break in favour of Paul and his supporters over the past five years. A critical turning point came in January 2013 when the one of Nova Scotia's leading historians, John Reid of Saint Mary's University, weighed in with an impeccably researched lecture and article published in the venerable *Journal of the Royal Nova Scotia Historical Society*. Reid's public lecture, entitled "The Three Lives of Edward Cornwallis," provided a reasonably fair, judicious and culturally responsive analysis of how historical reputations change over time.

(Left) Cover of Jon Tattrie's popular 2013 biography of Edward Cornwallis, a book that further fanned the public debate.

The early Cornwallis, Reid acknowledged, was a man of his time who established a small fortified town on the fringes of Mi'kmaki — a project that fell far short of his "imperial aspirations." The statue erected in 1931 by Canadian National Railways exemplified the Britannic Canadian spirit of the 1899 to 1949 period when "flagbearers" for Britannic civilization were commemorated and citizens celebrated the opening up of wider economic opportunities. From 1993 onward, with Paul's book animating discussion, Cornwallis emerged as an unsavoury and divisive figure, representing the atrocities associated with colonial dispossession and standing in the way of reconciliation.

BROKERING A DEAL

Growing protests from 2013 to 2016 and periodic acts of violence directed at the bronze statue kept the burning issue alive and eventually forced the hand of Halifax Mayor Mike Savage (son of Premier John Savage, who had advocated for Daniel Paul's book) and his city council. Downtown Halifax Councillor Waye Mason played an instrumental role, behind the scenes, attempting to find a compromise and broker a deal between the warring factions.

Periodic attempts by Halifax City Council to address the issue went for naught until April of 2017. Influenced by the message delivered by Mi'Kmaw poet Rebecca Thomas, recently-elected Halifax city councillor, Shawn Cleary, broke the impasse and succeeded in passing a resolution to call for a staff report. Eventually, it was decided to appoint an independent panel of experts charged with resolving the Cornwallis statue debacle and making recommendations related to public commemorations.

Appointing the Cornwallis Committee dragged on for months with temperatures rising on both sides. It reopened festering wounds as the factions jockeyed for control of the process. A confrontation erupted at the Cornwallis monument site in July 2017 and HRM draped a shroud around the statue to appease protestors threatening to take it down.

TAKING DOWN CORNWALLIS

The Assembly of Mi'kmaq Chiefs intervened in January 2018 expressing their displeasure with the delays and announced that they would "no longer participate in these panel discussions." They issued a public statement urging city council to "immediately" remove the statue and "deal with all commemorations of Cornwallis in HRM."

Within four days of that declaration, on January 30, 2018, the Mayor and Council moved to direct Halifax CAO Jacques Dube to proceed to "remove the statue of Edward Cornwallis" and to "place the statue in temporary storage" until such time as Council had "a long-term solution." The decision was made, according to the staff report, to avert a "risk to public safety" and to protect the public "reputation" of the city. The perceived threat to public safety was a protest planned for Sunday, February 4, 2018 when organizers planned to "bring down the Cornwallis statue."

City council was persuaded by HRM senior staff that the impending protest represented "a significant risk for damage to the statue, conflicts among protestors and counter-protestors and personal injury." Removing the statue was a hotly contested decision and one opposed, according to a CTV Atlantic News Poll, by 62 percent of some 2,872 poll respondents.

(Right) Statue of Edward Cornwallis being removed from its pedestal in South End Halifax after Halifax Regional Council voted to remove it from public view.

(Zane Woodford/ Star Metro) (Similar to ones shot by Darren Calabrese)

One day after the council vote, HRM staff arranged for the Cornwallis statue to be removed and transported to an undisclosed location. Television news footage and accompanying photographs captured the unceremonious lifting of the statue and the graphic images were beamed out and published across Canada and far beyond.

(Madeans/ Photograph by Darren Calabrese)

(Left) A crate reportedly containing the statue of Edward Cornwallis (inset) strapped on the top of a metal container was discovered in May 2018 in a Dartmouth municipal storage yard.

TOWARDS RECONCILIATION

Halifax instantly became known as a city that disowned its British colonial founder and publicly removed a monument commemorating its birth from the public square. On February 1, 2018, a group photo of Mayor Savage, Deputy Mayor Mason and Councillor Lorelei Nicoll, accompanied by National Assembly of First Nations Chief Perry Bellegarde and Mi'kmaw Regional Chief Morley Googoo, began circulating on social media. The National Chief was quoted as proclaiming the removal of the statue as a "great step" towards "reconciliation" with Canada's Indigenous peoples.

The Cornwallis statue was gone and in hiding, but not completely forgotten. Four months later an intrepid *Maclean's* magazine reporter uncovered the statue hidden from public view in Burnside Industrial Park across the harbour in Dartmouth. Behind a fence, surrounded by refuse and near a rusted-out oil tank, it was uncovered strapped atop two shipping containers and sealed inside a plywood box.

The promised Special Advisory Committee, co-chaired by museum curator Monica MacDonald and Chief Roderick Googoo, was finally announced in July 2018 and consisted of 10 members, including Daniel Paul and Professor John Reid.

Whether Edward Cornwallis was toppled or removed from his pedestal will be debated for years by citizens of Halifax and history buffs everywhere. Whatever is finally decided, it will likely reflect the closing words of advice offered in Reid's 2013 lecture: "Historical memory can and should evolve with each succeeding generation, and in our generation the integration of all three lives of Edward Cornwallis must form an important element of the evolution."

Digging Deeper – for Further Reading

Boileau, John, Bryan Elson, Len Canfield, and Leo J. Deveau, "Edward Cornwallis," Historical Paper No. 1, Halifax Military Heritage Preservation Society, November 28, 2016.

Deveau, Leo J., "Scrubbed, slanted history won't satisfy HRM visitors," The Chronicle Herald, May 26, 2018, E 3.

Paul, Daniel N., We Were Not the Savages: A Mi'kmaq Perspective on the Collision between European and Native American Civilizations. Twenty-First Century Edition. Halifax: Fernwood Publishers, 2000.

Reid, John G, "The Three Lives of Edward Cornwallis," Journal of the Royal Nova Scotia Historical Society, Vol. 16, 2013, pp. 19-45.

Tattrie, Jon, Cornwallis: The Violent Birth of Halifax. Lawrencetown, NS: Pottersfield Press, 2013.

Woodford, Zane, "Chairs say Halifax committee approaching Cornwallis issue with open minds," The Star Halifax, July 26, 2018.

Turning Point 15

Now or Never, Maybe:
The Ray Ivany Report and its Lessons, 2014 to Now

Speaking at Halifax's Pier 21 on Wednesday, February 12, 2014, Ray Ivany, Chair of the Nova Scotia Commission on Building Our New Economy, laid it on the line. The province, he stated, was "teetering on the brink of long-term decline" and the consequences would be dire if there was not a "dramatic shift" in attitudes and policies to address the demographic and economic realities.

That was the main thrust of Ivany's One Nova Scotia report, summarizing a year of public consultations, bearing the definitive title, *Now or Never: An Urgent Call to Action for Nova Scotians*. Five years later, that declaration still reverberates, but leaves many Nova Scotians wondering if the cold shower made any real difference.

'DIPPING IT IN IVANY'

Since that day, the Ivany Report has generated an amazing amount of public chatter and spin-off projects, ranging from the ONE Nova Scotia Coalition and Engage Nova Scotia to the weekly barrage of Now! Nova Scotia success stories. Most, if not all such ventures, were in the former Commission research director Mark Austin's memorable phrase "dipping it in Ivany" to capture public attention.

In spite of all the frenzied promotional activity, aside from the Syrian immigration boost, it's proving to be what Ivany promised — "a long slog." Our provincial budget, under the Stephen McNeil Liberal administration, is back in balance. Yet sifting through all the hype, and despite some herculean efforts, the trajectory does not indicate a significant change in direction.

Changing attitudes with 'Ivany magic' and stimulating more economic growth is far easier said than done. A Conference Board of Canada Outlook, released November 27, 2017, confirmed that Nova Scotia's economy stalled in 2017 with the second lowest provincial growth rate and is forecast to remain near the back of the pack for the next two years. After a 1.3 percent rise in real GDP in 2017, Nova Scotia is facing 1 percent growth in 2018, followed by 1.1 percent in 2019. That's in a national economy forecast to grow by 3.5 percent in 2017, 2.15 in 2018 and 1.8 percent in 2019.

The Ivany Report did not come out of nowhere. It was the Darrell Dexter NDP government's idea, but it drew upon the findings of earlier studies of the state of the Nova Scotia economy and regional economic development. Upon taking office in 2009, Dexter and his chief policy advisor Rick Williams sought economic advice from a panel of experts, including New Brunswick public administration specialist Donald Savoie, president of the Atlantic Provinces Economic Council Elizabeth Beale, Dalhousie University economist Lars Osberg and former BMO executive-turned-consultant Tim O'Neill.

The Panel of Economic Advisors weighed in in November 2009 with an economic storm warning. They reported to Dexter that Nova Scotia faced a $1.4-billion structural deficit by 2014 and the looming crisis called for what Williams dubbed "a three-legged stool" approach to restoring economic health: exercise spending discipline, restrain public-sector wage growth and raise revenues by reclaiming the federal government's two percent cut to the HST.

Dexter and his cabinet, acting on Williams' advice, were convinced that austerity alone would not break the cycle of slow growth. The leading expert on Atlantic regional development, Savoie, offered a piece of sage advice — you cannot ask people to tackle a problem they don't know they have.

ONE NOVA SCOTIA

ONE NS DASHBOARD

A dashboard of objective, reliable data on our collective progress toward the ONE NS goals. **Learn More**

(One Nova Scotia NS/ www.onens.ca)

SHIPS START HERE

Securing the massive federal shipbuilding contract spawned a Halifax-centric development strategy, spearheaded by the Halifax Chamber of Commerce and the Halifax Partnership, aimed at affirming Halifax as a "gateway city" and anchored by a city booster campaign with the slogan, "Jobs Start Here." It was also packaged for promotional purposes as "Ships Start Here."

While Donald Savoie was working on strengthening regional development and applying a "rural lens" to seed local initiatives outside Halifax, the Dexter government secured the $25-billion Irving shipbuilding contract in October 2011 and opted to build everything around the Jobs Start Here agenda.

The Jobs Here strategy simply did not work in giving the NDP government what, according to Williams, it was really looking for: "a political bounce" in the polls. Losing three paper mills in 2012 in quick succession inflicted economic damage on Port Hawkesbury, Liverpool and Hantsport, further damaging the government's reputation for promoting more growth.

Enter Ray Ivany, President of Acadia University and a dynamic, growth-positive educational administrator. Fresh from building the showpiece Nova Scotia Community College Dartmouth Waterfront Campus, he appeared to have a Midas touch for turning around people and organizations.

While Savoie had recommended a more robust rural development strategy, Ivany adopted a different approach, right from the beginning. He accepted the challenge of chairing the commission on condition that it promoted what Williams now describes as "a Halifax city-state" strategy. He insisted that the project focus on "building one economy," operate at arms-length from the government and have a longer reporting timeline, which turned out to be after an impending election.

Ivany rejected the popular assumption, shared by Savoie, that there were "two Nova Scotia's" on either side of an urban-rural divide. He set out to challenge established ideas and perceptions, including this ingrained notion: "If it's good for Halifax, it's not necessarily good for the rest of Nova Scotia."

The Acadia University president assembled a team of four commissioners, including the Oxford blueberry industry king John Bragg, and conducted a province-wide round of 'world café' consultations. All the lead presentations rang the alarm bell about the impending fiscal and demographic crisis, but tried to strike an upbeat we-shall-overcome tone. Everywhere he stopped, Ivany drew attention to a 'point of light,' such as Honeycrisp apples in the Annapolis Valley.

After alerting Nova Scotians to the fiscal and demographic cliff ahead, the Ivany report attempted to set a positive sense of direction. It identified a few ways to address key issues holding the province back and proposed 10-year "stretch goals," focusing on increased immigration, expanded export sales, support for business start-ups and modernization of traditional resource industries.

(Top) "Ships Start Here" was the slogan of a Halifax-driven business initiative that captured the spirit of the Ivany report.

'GAME CHANGERS'

Ivany identified what were termed "game changers" holding out promise for the future. Among his favourite examples of the bright lights were High Liner Foods, Oxford Frozen Foods, Clearwater Seafoods, Jost Vineyards, Membertou First Nation and Cabot Links Golf Course.

Ivany and his team conveyed a sense of urgency. "When you are hanging on the edge," he told reporters, "you don't say, 'let's make a slight move to the left or the right.' You turn and get back on solid ground and keep going."

Yarmouth Mayor Pam Mood was effusive in her support for the Ivany initiative. "Most of us arrived on different ships," she said at the Pier 21 announcement. "We're all on the same boat now… and it's all hands on deck." Ivany commissioner Susanna Fuller was more measured about the potential turn-around. "We are," she quipped, "getting to 'maybe,' and away from 'no.'"

The Ivany Report generated incredible media coverage and that exerted considerable pressure on Premier McNeil and his relatively new government. Since it was not his initiative, the Premier responded rather cautiously. McNeil was, he said, "encouraged" by the report, but rather non-committal in response to reporter's questions: "We, as a government, I think, have to send a (message) that we're setting the table, and we need the private sector to actually create the jobs."

(Michael De ADDER, The Chronicle Herald)

(Left) The Premier and the Report: Stephen MacNeil appears to have shelved the Ivany Report in this satirical cartoon, published in September of 2014.

THE 10-YEAR PLAN

The McNeil government rejected a proposed "all-party government alliance" in support of the Ivany Report, and took four months before establishing a ONE Nova Scotia Coalition to translate the proposed goals into actionable plans. Guided by Rankin MacSween of Sydney, Cape Breton, the coalition was tasked to develop and deliver a 10-year, province-wide plan to meet population and economic renewal goals.

After creating the 15-member Coalition on June 2, 2014, three more months passed without any visible action whatsoever. Alarmed by the loss of momentum and what he described as a "deafening silence," Halifax's leading pollster, Don Mills, produced his own seven-step business-friendly plan to kick start the sputtering economy. The Mills prescription took up Ivany's challenge and called for these actions: 1) youth retention through payroll rebates; 2) triple foreign student enrollments; 3) increase the population; 4) create urban-centred economic zones; 5) create an entrepreneurial environment; 6) rebalance the public sector-dominated workforce; and 7) improve regulations to allow for resource development.

Rural development advocates and agencies were sidelined by the Ivany Report. Like the One Nova Scotia Commission, the Coalition was metropolitan-centric and committed to export-driven growth rather than local enterprise-driven regional development. Successive proposals from the Nova Scotia Smalls Schools Initiative calling for a rural development strategy and local revitalization through community-school hub development went nowhere.

'AUSTERITY AGENDA'

Local business initiatives seeded by Community Economic Development (CED) agencies were essentially dismissed by Ivany as insufficient in meeting the steep challenge. While such efforts demonstrated "energies, resilience and creativity," the report claimed that they would not be the "dominant component" of provincial economic strategy. Tapping into social enterprise potential, proposed by David Upton of Common Good Solutions, eventually cracked through by sheer persistence and eventually got a fair hearing with the Coalition and provincial business promotion agencies.

Ivany Commission research lead Mark Austin laments what happened in the aftermath of the report. Seeking to balance the provincial budget, the McNeil government narrowed the focus down to the three-legged stool approach, pursuing government austerity and public-sector wage restraint. Local enterprise development took a definite backseat to reining in spending on public sector wages and benefits.

The McNeil government (2013-17) did act upon the Ivany austerity agenda and continued to pursue what St. Francis Xavier political scientist Peter Clancy described as a neo-liberal fiscal plan. To rein in public expenditures, McNeil and his cabinet enacted a series of three bills aimed at restructuring the health sector bargaining framework as well as imposing essential service regulations. They also maintained a hard fiscal stance on public-sector settlements from 2013 to 2016, giving the teachers (NSTU) and government employees (NSGEU) a multi-year wage freeze followed by annual increments of 1.0, 1.5 and 0.5 percent. In December of 2015, McNeil's

Liberals unveiled *Public Services Sustainability Act*, employing it as a tool in limiting wage increase increments and top-up retirement allowances. The strategy harkened back to the wage limits imposed by the Savage government in the 1990s.

Tightening our belts and "doing less of the same old thing" will not, in Austin's view, "create the new economy." What is really needed is a commitment to build upon "social assets" rather than "choking off infrastructure."

"The alternative to austerity isn't wastefulness," he told CBC Radio's Mainstreet, "it's resourcefulness. Rural Nova Scotia has it in abundance."

The ONE Nova Scotia "Playbook," released November 6, 2015, merely reaffirmed the direction set in Ivany's report and attempted to put some flesh on the bones of the province-wide economic action plan. Piled on top of the 10 initial goals was the Collaborative Action Plan comprising 58 specific recommendations in seven broad areas, demonstrating that universities, early learning and ocean industries have come out on top.

ALL FOR ONE NOVA SCOTIA?

The seven Coalition priorities, to be specific, were: providing the youngest Nova Scotians with the best start in life; stemming the persistent out-migration of our youth; attracting and retaining more immigrants; supporting 'regional innovation hubs' centred on university and college towns; equipping Nova Scotia to be an information technology leader in Canada, thereby fostering more globally-competitive export businesses; and fully exploiting our many ocean-related advantages.

The initial allure of Ivany's vision definitely wore-off, particularly in the groves of academe, the incubators of social enterprise and the swath of Nova Scotia outside Halifax. That was very much in evidence at a lively and revealing September 19, 2017 panel presentation, hosted by Kevin Quigley's Dalhousie University MacEachen Institute and billed as "All for One Nova Scotia? Perspectives on the Ivany Report."

Two of the architects of the ONE Nova Scotia economic development agenda, senior NDP advisor Williams and former Liberal leader Danny Graham, now heading Engage Nova Scotia, offered up explanations for the policy choices made in Ivany's report and the subsequent ONE Nova Scotia "Playbook" embraced since November 2015 by McNeil's government.

As a senior advisor to the McNeil government, Graham was now advocating the adoption of the Genuine Progress Index (GPI), first proposed in 2007 by community health expert Ron Colman. It's an attempt to introduce an alternative to the growth model of progress that measures income distribution as one of its 22 core social, economic and environmental components. Increases in poverty and inequality are seen in the GPI as a loss in social capital. Advocates of this approach claim that promoting equity, reducing poverty and increasing food security are associated with improved economic performance and social stability.

(Opposite) Welcoming Immigrants: The Ivany Report urged Nova Scotians to be more welcoming of immigrants because the province faced a serious demographic decline in the years ahead. Here, Jackie and Raj Fernando, originally from Sri Lanka, pose in February 2014 with their son, Adrian, at Chebucto Grocery, Halifax.

focus on boosting population and increasing economic development.

Here are some of them, with the idea of implementation or getting close by 2024:

- business startups.
- Increase annual export value by 50 per cent to more than $20 billion.
- Youth employment rate at or better than the national rate.

- A commitment to finding sustainable and value-added approaches for traditional industries.
- Reform of municipal government and regional service structures.

...divide and jurisdictional fighting.

Source: Now or Never: An Urgent Call to Action for Nova Scotians

N.S. urged to welcome immigrants

Ivany report finds some in province still feel newcomers may threaten their jobs

SELENA ROSS
STAFF REPORTER

✉ sross@herald.ca
🐦 @CH_sross

Nova Scotia needs to get its act together when it comes to immigrants, Ray Ivany found.

"Nova Scotians appear to be very positive about newcomers from other parts of Canada but somewhat less welcoming to immigrants," says the report, which came out of a commission the Acadia University president chaired.

"There is a segment of the population that believes that immigrants take away jobs from other Nova Scotians. Rural residents appear to be more concerned than their urban counterparts on this issue."

The commission, tasked with looking at Nova Scotia's economic future, learned about people's attitudes through survey research.

It found that, contrary to those beliefs, immigrants to Nova Scotia are often success stories. Their unemployment rate is 7.4 per cent, compared with 10 per cent for immigrants across Canada.

Fewer than 20 per cent of non-immigrant Nova Scotians have a university education, while 42 per cent of immigrants to the province do.

"All of us can look around and see examples of how recent flows

Jackie Fernando, husband Raj and son Adrian, 12, at Chebucto Grocery in Halifax. The Fernandos are originally from Sri Lanka. **TIM KROCHAK ▪ Staff**

less than one-third of the rates across other provinces. The Ivany commission set a goal of nearly tripling the annual average of 2,400 new immigrants who become permanent residents.

That will require the co-operation of the federal government, which controls immigration

...fessional and trade credentials to simply becoming more hospitable, said the report.

"Nova Scotians everywhere — in their communities, educational settings and workplaces — need to demonstrate that we are an open and welcoming society so that our

arrived in Nova Scotia from Sri Lanka two decades ago, sponsored by her sister.

Now Fernando owns a convenience store in Halifax's west end. She has found the city welcoming, she said, adding that cultural associations are important.

ROOM FOR MORE?

Federal Justice Minister Peter MacKay says he supports giving Nova Scotia more room to bring in immigrants.

For years, provinces have been pushing for more room under the provincial nominee program, but Ottawa has been reluctant to raise the overall number of immigrants coming into Canada.

"It depends," MacKay said. "We obviously have to have a system that's fair, a system that's safe. They have to do it in a calibrated way with the provinces."

Despite previous rejections, MacKay said he believes it is possible Citizenship and Immigration Minister Chris Alexander could give the provinces more nominee spaces.

they have a place for you here in Nova Scotia."

Another factor is the ease of studying, she said. Many new immigrants of all ages want to attend local universities, but working their way through school

(MacEachen Institute for Public Policy and Governance, Dalhousie University)

(Left) Senior NDP policy advisor Rick Williams speaking at the MacEachen Institute Panel on the Ivany Report, September 19, 2017.

THE PLAN AND ITS CRITICS

Two Dalhousie professors, historian Jerry Bannister and sociologist Karen Foster, had a field day picking apart the Ivany Report's analysis and core strategy. Surveying the Ivany Report's interpretation of recent Nova Scotia history, Bannister found it to be narrowly focused on economic indicators, offering a singular cycle of decline narrative and presenting "history drained of politics." Little or no reference was made in the report to Indigenous perspectives or the Antigonish cooperative local development movement. He also found it strange the Ivany Report's economic history had "no villains" because there were "no competing narratives" to be found in the story.

Professor Foster challenged directly the Ivany Report's core assumptions and almost exclusive focus on promoting economic growth at the expense of other priorities. She was troubled by the report's focus on "attitudes about economic development" and its unrelenting advocacy of "ONE-ness" in the form of a "shared vision and commitment to economic growth." Class divisions, income inequalities and the survival of rural communities, she claims, have been written out of the province's future. The great irony of the Ivany Report and its framing of public discussion, is, in Foster's words: "The blame is laid locally, but the placeless solutions erase the local."

More and more Nova Scotians are wondering if the Ivany Report prescription is really the only way to grow our economy. One of its architects, Rick Williams, seems to be having second thoughts. Since the release of the report, he's come to realize, more than ever, that "Halifax is not Nova Scotia" and a growing capital does not translate into better times outside Halifax. In that sense, Savoie was more accurate than Ivany in his assessment.

Digging Deeper – for Further Reading

All for One Nova Scotia: Perspectives on the Ivany Report. Panel Discussion, MacEachen Institute for Public Policy and Governance. Kevin Quigley, Moderator, September 19, 2017.

Austin, Mark, "Rural Reckoning: Find value in our place and our people," CBC News Nova Scotia, September 30, 2015.

Foster, Karen, Productivity and Prosperity: A Historical Sociology of Productivist Thought. Toronto: University of Toronto Press, 2016.

Ivany, Ray, The Report of the Nova Scotia Commission on Building Our New Economy. Halifax: OneNS.ca, February 2014.

Macdonald, Andrew, "Don Mills' Economic Rescue Plan would fix ailing Rural Nova Scotia," The Macdonald Report, May 5, 2018.

Mills, Don, "7 ways to pull start cord on a sputtering province," The Chronicle Herald, August 30, 2014. F4. ONE Nova Scotia Coalition, We Choose Now – A Playbook for Nova Scotians. Halifax: wechoosenow.ca, November 2015.

One Nova Scotia: Progress at the Half-Way Mark, Goal Progress Summary. Halifax: Government of Nova Scotia, February 2019.

WHERE ARE WE NOW?

Five years after the Ivany Report, the One Nova Scotia Commission implementation team issued an optimistic report testifying to the progress made in achieving the plan's goals. The Stephen McNeil government took pride in reporting in February 2019 that the province's population was growing, unemployment was down, immigration numbers were up, and business innovation underway in the oceans and tech sectors. That mid-term (5-year) government report claimed that the province had made progress on half of the original goals. In spite of such claims, skeptics remained who pointed to the province's relative economic growth and productivity performance in relation to other North American jurisdictions.

A recent Corporate Research Associates analysis, prepared by Don Mills, confirmed in 2017 that not much had changed for Nova Scotia since the Ivany Report. Growth in GDP bottomed out in 2012 and 2013, but still languished at around 1 percent and averaged only 0.7 percent over the past decade, besting only New Brunswick and Newfoundland and Labrador.

With support for the Ivany agenda flagging, Mills stepped up his advocacy for a regional economic hubs strategy. In a series of speeches and a new Halifax Chronicle Herald column from 2017 until 2019, he made the case for a rural Nova Scotia economic rescue plan. Concerned about the fact that 43 per cent of Nova Scotians lived in declining rural communities of under 5,000 people, he proposed a much more robust regional development strategy focused on "townsizing" or growing the eight sizeable towns outside Halifax stretching from Yarmouth to Sydney, Cape Breton.

Confronting those economic realities and the Conference Board forecast for 2017 to 2019, all bets were off on economic growth recovery any time soon. Nova Scotia still has the potential, if only we could find a way to unlock it in the years ahead. Creating new measures of success, such as GPI Atlantic's proposed Quality of Life Index, might provide a useful measure of our total health and vitality. Whether Mills' regional hubs strategy would gain traction remained to be seen. Creating private-sector jobs remains a clear priority and we are still searching for a strategy capable of producing winning conditions going forward.

Acknowledgements

Nova Scotia's provincial newspaper, *The Chronicle Herald*, founded in 1874, has a history that is intertwined with pivotal episodes that shaped the destiny of the province. Like its rival paper, the Halifax *Morning Chronicle* (1827-1907), the *Herald* produced the 'first draft of history' with its news reportage, editorials, and features. So, it was fitting that, 150 years after Confederation, the *Herald* editors dedicated a whole section, *NovaScotian*, to commemorating historic milestones, notables, and achievements. That decision opened the door to the publication of my 12- part series of "Turning Points" features which ran weekly from September to December 2017. Might I thank, first and foremost, my editors, Colleen Cosgrove and Paul O'Connell, for your critical roles in supporting this ambitious venture and the re-publication of the series of features. Library Manager at the Herald, Debbie Reid, also helped greatly in accessing vintage photo illustrations.

Initial inspiration for the whole concept came from the response of my former Grade 10 history students at Halifax Grammar School. The introductory unit of my Canadian history course, "Joe Howe's Canada," captured their interest because it approached the Confederation years through a unique Nova Scotian lens. Seeing my students' eyes bulge while watching the ferocious public debates over Confederation featured in the old NFB film classic, "*Charles Tupper: The Big Man*," remains a vivid memory. That's why it ended up as the first turning point in the series.

Popular history books like this one are constructed on the foundations laid by historians, newspaper editors, and non-fiction authors before them. Each chapter in the book provides a short list of the key works on each of the topics. Nova Scotian authors John DeMont and Lesley Choyce, as well as historian Ian McKay contributed much to my understanding of the big picture. Reading the book, you will quickly see the immense debt that I owe to well-respected historians such as Peter B. Waite, Colin D. Howell, Brian D. Tennyson, Margaret Conrad, Ernie Forbes, and Tina Loo. Later chapters rely heavily on insights gleaned from the writings of Dalton Camp, Wanda Robson, Peter Clancy, Daniel N. Paul, Jon Tattrie, Howard Epstein, and Don Mills.

My publisher, John MacIntyre, and book editor, Vernon Oickle, deserve a hearty thanks for believing in the book and for effectively shepherding it through to publication. You treat your authors with respect and that allowed me ample scope to shape and enrich the book. The attractive design, imaginative layout, and profuse illustrations are the work of Denis Cunningham and a testament to his many talents. Thanks, as well, to Chris Benjamin for copy-editing the book.

Last, but not least, I want to thank Dianne, a truly amazing woman who has been my constant companion and biggest supporter all these years. She is not only my enabler, but the one who brings me down to earth when I'm chasing the next big idea, accumulating mountains of research, or flying off in all directions. It is to her that I dedicate this book.

Paul W. Bennett
March 2, 2019

Index